CW01464075

Joe Arrived Dead

The Birth of a Yorkshire Coal Town

Hemsworth 1860-1910

John Lynas

First published on the 18th of January 2007 by St Sulpice Books
356, Sharrow Lane, Sheffield.
1st edition

Order this book online at www.trafford.com/07-0626
or email orders@trafford.com

Most Trafford titles are also available at major online book retailers.

Note for Librarians: A cataloguing record for this book is available from Library and Archives Canada at www.collectionscanada.ca/amicus/index-e.html

ISBN: 978-1-4251-6858-2

We at Trafford believe that it is the responsibility of us all, as both individuals and corporations, to make choices that are environmentally and socially sound. You, in turn, are supporting this responsible conduct each time you purchase a Trafford book, or make use of our publishing services. To find out how you are helping, please visit www.trafford.com/responsiblepublishing.html

Our mission is to efficiently provide the world's finest, most comprehensive book publishing service, enabling every author to experience success. To find out how to publish your book, your way, and have it available worldwide, visit us online at www.trafford.com/10510

www.trafford.com

North America & international
toll-free: 1 888 232 4444 (USA & Canada)
phone: 250 383 6864 • fax: 250 383 6804 • email: info@trafford.com

The United Kingdom & Europe
phone: +44 (0)1865 722 113 • local rate: 0845 230 9601
facsimile: +44 (0)1865 722 868 • email: info.uk@trafford.com

10 9 8 7 6 5 4 3

This writing is based on research of primary sources and discussions over a period of many years with the older inhabitants of Hemsworth, Kinsley and Fitzwilliam.

Photographs used have been copied from the originals held by residents of this area who have given permission for them to be copied.

Table of Contents

Introduction

The township of Hemsworth snuggles peacefully in the middle of the triangle formed by the Yorkshire towns of Barnsley, Doncaster and Pontefract. It was recorded in the Doomsday as an agricultural community, an identity it retained until the industrial revolution and the discovery of coal in that part of Yorkshire.

The insatiable demand for fuel to feed the home fires and furnaces of the developing industries gave rise to an intensive search for new sources of good quality coal.

Yorkshire's excellent coal seams, the Barnsley Bed, the Haigh Moor and Shafton seams were known to run near the town. However it took the courage of Richard Fosdick, a dealer on the London Coal Exchange to locate and recover coal from these seams within the boundaries of the township.

Fosdick leased land from the Fitzwilliam family, located all three seams of coal, and so began a chain of events which completely changed the landscape and the township of Hemsworth.

From today's perspective Hemsworth appears to be *just another small mining community in Yorkshire,* though the history of the people who made up the community shows a deeply engrained radical, social and political culture which set it apart from other townships within the Yorkshire coalfield.

This book attempts to cover the main changes in the Town between 1876 and 1910, an era during which Hemsworth, including the villages of Kinsley and the new estate we know as Fitzwilliam, changed qualitatively.

Unfortunately one cannot look at this period in the history of Hemsworth without covering the great strike; however I have attempted to do so from the perspective of the local collier and his family. By this, I mean that whilst it is necessary to identify and describe the role of the Yorkshire Miners Association and the Yorkshire Coal Owners Association when examining any dispute in any Yorkshire colliery, I have concentrated much more on the inhabitants of the township and their tremendous organisational skills and ingenuity.

To this end I have tried wherever possible to use the names of the key players in the Township as well as identify the names of as many of the ordinary men, women and children who participated and whose names were recorded in the journals and newspapers of the time, primarily because it is their story.

This part of the history ends with the colliery being purchased by the Shaw family and re-opened as part of their coal mining empire. With this came the official end of the strike, refurbishment of some of the houses in Kinsley and the building of the new houses at Fitzwilliam; a series of events which heralded a period of stability and growth for this quiet, yet important, mining town.

I have included a section on the negotiations between mining families seeking assistance from the Hemsworth Board of Guardians to remind us of the conditions our ancestors had to endure before the advent of the welfare state.

In a similar vein, three poems scratched on the doors of the Paupers cells in the Hemsworth Poor House are reproduced to provide us with a glimpse of the feelings of some of the unfortunate residents in this facility.

The Main Players

John Potts was the acknowledged leader of the Hemsworth and Kinsley miners. According to 'Whose Who of British Members of Parliament Vol 111':

'John Potts, son of Robert Potts (coal miner) and Mary Kirkman, born on August the 12th 1861 in Bolton, Lancashire.'

The Potts family moved to Durham and at eleven years of age John was employed as a surface worker at Sacriston Colliery where he worked for approximately eight years before moving to Stargate Colliery, Newcastle, working there for a further year. During this early period of employment in the pits he passed through all types of underground work including *coal-hewer.*

Returning to Yorkshire as a youth, in the late 1870's he took up employment as *coal-hewer* at the Hemsworth Colliery and at 29 years of age was elected to the position of *checkweighman* at the Shafton seam.

During the notorious Parliamentary election in Barnsley in 1897, (in which the Independent Labour Candidate Pete Curran was stoned by colliers), Potts was a nominee of the victorious Liberal Candidate, Sir Joseph Walton.

A Wesleyan Methodist lay preacher and advocate of temperance, John Potts was always willing to fight for his beliefs. For example, in 1904:

'The Reverend Henry Taylor and Mr John Potts suffered restraint on their goods rather than pay that portion of the Poor Rate which they held went towards sectarian teaching in schools.'

Whilst in Hemsworth he lived in Holly Bank with his wife and two sons. Potts was a prominent activist in Local Government, Education and the Yorkshire Miners Association. With the passing of the Local Government Act of 1894 he became Leader of the Labour Group. He served for almost 30 years on Parish Council, Rural Council, School Boards, Board of Guardians and West Riding County Council and was a Justice of the Peace in Barnsley. An elected member of the Joint Board of Owners and Workmen, John Potts was acknowledged expert on Miners Pay and Conditions; he was called to give evidence on behalf of the Miners Federation of Great Britain to the Sankey Coal Commission on the probability of reduced working hours leading to a reduction in workplace accidents. John Potts was a Member of Parliament for Barnsley from November 1922 until October 1931 when he was defeated. He was re-elected in November 1935 and remained as M.P. until his death.

During the Hemsworth dispute Potts inspired and captivated audiences with his passion and attention to detail, he was not however noted for his parliamentary speeches. He did introduce the *'Employers Liability Bill'* on the floor of the House of Commons which was defeated.

Following a long illness he died on the 28th of April 1938 at his home in Carlton near Barnsley.

His contribution to society was summarised in the South Yorkshire Times of May 16th 1938:

'In his fiery youth Mr Potts was a great agitator with a keen brain and a sharp tongue. His controversial powers were tempered in the fires of the terrible Hemsworth Coal Strike. Some of his best

public and industrial work was done in that district before he came to Barnsley to take over the treasurership of the Yorkshire Miners Association... he was to the miners always a champion of their rights and a tireless worker in their interests. He went to Parliament 20 years too late to be effective there. He made no great figure and spoke rarely though he must at times felt himself in the presence of his own youth renewed as he listened to Mr George Griffiths one of the younger Hemsworth school launching his wit at the Government Benches. Truly he has worn himself out in the cause of the workers from whom he sprang.'

Note: George Griffiths was not involved in the Hemsworth dispute. Originally from Flintshire, George Griffiths moved to Royston near Barnsley in Yorkshire in 1903. He was elected as the Member of Parliament for the Hemsworth constituency following the mysterious drowning of Gabriel Price M.P. for Hemsworth in 1934.

Sources: Neville's unpublished thesis. Joyce Bellamy, Biography of Labour Leaders, Barnsley Chronicle.

Gabriel Price: M.P. for Hemsworth from 1931 until his death in 1934.

Gabriel Price, often referred to as Gabe, was born in Fairburn near Castleford in 1879. At twelve years of age he completed his education at Hemsworth Boys Church School and started work in the Hemsworth Colliery. A keen sportsman, Gabe played rugby for Kinsley, Dewsbury and Yorkshire County. On the 30th of April 1901 Gabriel married Winifred Watson of Hemsworth.

During the strike he became treasurer of the *Nipsey Fund*, in this capacity his attention to detail allied with his insistence on transparency and accountability ensured that all money collected or donated to the fund were recorded and published for all to see. This insistence on accountability resulted in the attempted prosecution of two members of the strike relief committee plus the prosecution and jailing of one collector found guilty of misappropriating *Nipsey* collections.

Gabriel Price appears to have got involved in 'Politics' during the strike when he became a regular speaker at the Wednesday meetings of the Independent Labour Party. After the Hemsworth dispute Gabe went on to become president of the Frickley branch of the Yorkshire Miners Association. By 1913 his political activities led to his appointment to the Hemsworth Board of Guardians, then election to serve as a member of the West Riding County Council in 1919, and Chairman of Hemsworth District Rural Council. He subsequently became a Justice of the Peace and a member of the Board of Governors of Sheffield University; the following year he became an Alderman of the County. In 1931 Gabriel was elected as Member of Parliament for Hemsworth, a position he held for a mere three years before his untimely death by drowning in 1934.

Isaac Burns: Miners Leader, was born in Cumberland, one of twelve children in the family Isaac began his working life at the age of 12 when he was employed in the Iron mines near Barrow in Furness.

At the age of 21 he moved to South Yorkshire and found employment in South Kirkby Colliery where he worked for a short time before packing his bags and heading to the United States of America. Here he worked for around four years in the Copper, Silver and Gold mines of Arizona, Oklahoma, Colorado and Montana, where, in his own words, he was:

'Often down but never out.'

In 1895 he returned to Yorkshire and Hemsworth where he again found employment in the South Kirkby Colliery. A devout Roman Catholic, Ike was a committed family man who refrained from drinking and smoking to ensure a good education and life style for his family.

Known throughout the labour movement as Ike, Burns was a flamboyant character who had the distinction of being one of the first socialists among the South Yorkshire miners well known for:

'Flaunting rather than wearing his flaming red tie.'

During the infamous Barnsley by-election of 1897 in which Pete Curran the socialist candidate was stoned by the miners, Curran resided at the Hemsworth home of Isaac and his family.

Although employed at South Kirkby Colliery, Ike worked closely with the Hemsworth strike committee organising collections and criticising Y.M.A. branch officials for not giving support to the Hemsworth families. As a School Manager he was a key figure in the debates with the Local Board of Guardians on the question of feeding the miner's children. His political activity enabled him to be one of the first Labour members to be elected to the Hemsworth

District Council. Indeed many of his contemporaries thought he was one of the best miner's leaders not to be elected to parliament.

Chapter One

Birth of a Colliery

Work on the Hemsworth Main Colliery was begun in the first quarter of 1876 by the Fitzwilliam Hemsworth Colliery Company. Richard Fosdick, a prominent member of the London Coal Exchange who represented the Stafford Colliery near Barnsley, created this vehicle to search for the valuable coal seams known to run through this part of Yorkshire. Mr Fosdick commenced his search for coal in the village of Kinsley which is part of the township of Hemsworth. On land leased from the Earl of Fitzwilliam he commenced exploratory sinking operations to find the financially lucrative Barnsley Bed and the Shafton and Haigh Moor seams of coal so much in demand to fuel the fires of transport and industry.

The opening of the exploratory shaft in this area was encouraged and greatly assisted by the development of the railway system in this part of Yorkshire, which was heralded by the opening of the railway station in the nearby village of Cudworth:

'On the Hull and Grimsby Branch of the Great Northern Railway Company.'

The railway system provided an efficient low cost method of transporting bulky and heavy goods such as coal, thereby providing access and opening up the market place.

Mr Fosdick's apparent gamble paid dividends. A short time after commencing work on the exploratory shaft, one local newspaper proudly announced:

'After sinking operations extending over a year and a quarter, an excellent seam of coal has been won at the Hemsworth Main Colliery in a part of the coal field where the measures have not hitherto been worked. The finding of a good seam of coal, five feet in thickness, and at a depth of only rather over 140 yards, is a proceeding of which the owner might well feel proud, as he has been the means of opening out what may be termed a maiden coal field. The seam (sic) is the Shafton Bed of which a thousand acres has been leased from one of the leading landowners, whilst a further area is within easy reach. The shafts are within a short distance of a railway, which will afford ample means of forwarding the produce to all the leading markets. Another advantage is that there is no colliery in the locality, so that a good deal of land sale will be secured. A land shaft is in the course of sinking, and this, when opened out, will form a somewhat extensive concern. A splendid surface plant, together with winding engines and other appliances, will be provided, so that when properly developed, the colliery will be able to yield from 700 to 800 tons per day.'

As the pit shaft and underground roadways were opened out to provide access to the whole of the Shafton seam, the colliery provided work for:

'Almost 200 men and boys, using candles to light up their underground workplace.'

Although the employment of boys was common in collieries at

this time, legislation did impose some limits on the age and type of work they could be employed on. Mr Fosdick, in common with many other colliery owners of the time, did not always adhere to the requirements of this legislation. As a consequence of ignoring these laws, at Barnsley Court on the 20th of July 1877:

'Richard Fosdick owner of Hemsworth Main Colliery now being opened out was charged by Mr Beaumont factory inspector with employing 3 lads, Thomas Wroe, Edwin Booty and John Hawley. Wroe aged 8 was employed in the brickyard whilst the other 2 both aged 13 were employed at the colliery.'

The court imposed a fine of 20 shillings plus costs in the case of Wroe, and 10 shillings plus costs for the other two lads.

Having been successful in finding and recovering coal from the Shafton seam, sinking work continued to gain access to the deeper but financially more lucrative Barnsley and Haigh Moor seams much in demand by heavy industry. The search did not take long, in January 1878 the Wakefield Express reported:

'Although great difficulties have had to be overcome in the sinking of the new Fitzwilliam Hemsworth Colliery – fair progress is being made. The coal was won in one shaft some time ago and a second shaft is within 30 yards of the coal. A good deal of water has had to be contended with and the undertaking is looked on as one likely to be not only remunerative but valuable.'

The brick yard in which young Wroe was employed had been opened to provide materials for constructing the colliery offices and ancillary buildings, as well as terraced cottages for the colliery workers. The first of these long rows of collier's houses was completed in 1878 at a total cost of £4,000 for 30 houses, or £133-7s-6d per house.

The houses, designed by the architect James Hindle, were built by *Crowther Brothers,* a local company owned and run by Edward Laffette-Balfe and Henry William Crowther. A disagreement developed between architect and builders as to what was contained in the specification of the houses. Hindle, the Architect, claimed the doors had been fitted on the wrong side and no handrail had been provided on the steps up to the attic. Consequently he refused to issue a certificate of work done; this effectively prevented the builders being paid for work already completed. *Crowther Brothers* had carried out work to the value of £3,600 and received payment of £1,916. Balfe had written to Fosdick's solicitors several times, pointing out that his company had met the architect's original specification and were thus entitled to payment in full; no response had been received. Matters came to a head on the 13th of April when Richard Fosdick and James Hindle visited the houses to inspect progress.

In his rush to have the houses built and occupied as quickly as possible Fosdick tolerated no delays. He advised the builder that he would like to move his colliers into the houses on the following Monday.

'Balfe agreed they would be ready for occupation by that date but refused to hand over possession until all the houses were certified (sic). A scuffle ensued between architect and builder during which Hindle tried to throw Balfe out of one of the houses. Being unsuccessful in his attempts, the architect resorted to locking the builder inside one of his houses. As a consequence, James Hindle was duly charged with assaulting Edward Balfe and appeared at Barnsley magistrates court where he was fined 20/- plus costs of £1-15s-6d.'

On the same day, in the same court, John Webster, William Ball, Walter Greenfield and William Benson, colliers employed at Hemsworth Main Colliery, were charged with breaking four squares of glass. During the court hearing it became evident that Fosdick decided to move his workers into the houses:

'Fosdick asked the builder to give up possession, Balfe refused, the men then started to move their possessions into the houses, taking out glass and in one case a door lock to get entry.'

Webster, Ball, Greenfield, and Benson were all found guilty and fined 5 shillings plus costs and damages; Fosdick paid the men's fines, costs and damages.

Whilst Balfe and his company won that particular battle they lost the war, a few months later a meeting of the creditors of Edward Laffette-Balfe and Mr Henry William Crowther trading as *Crowther Brothers* agreed to allow the company to go into voluntary liquidation with debts amounting to £2,401-11s-8d and assets valued at £1,275.

The first reported death at the colliery was recorded on the 31st of August 1878. Richard Hancock, aged 13, a screen worker, was crushed to death between two wagons on the pithead.

The economic depression of the late 1870s had affected most industries, however its effect on capital intensive industries was crippling.

The ramifications of the depression hit the Hemsworth colliery workers in Early May 1879. By the 10th of May all the employees, both pit and brick yard workers, received two weeks notice to leave work. Up to this point the colliery had been working every day, drawing good coal which sold easily in London.

On receiving notices terminating their employment at the colliery miners began to move away from the area, however many had grievances over the date of issue of the notices and preferred to remain and contest the issue with their former employer.

Because of their actions and negotiations with Richard Fosdick the notices were re-issued with the proper date, however for some reason, I have been unable to establish precisely why, William Franklin, Enoch Davenport and John Arnold were instructed to leave the pit immediately.

A meeting of between three and four hundred men and boys employed by the Colliery Company was hastily organised on Kinsley Common. At this meeting the miners agreed no one would return to work until the three men named previously had also been re-instated. Subsequently a deputation from the miners met with Fosdick and Bennet, the colliery manager, to try and resolve the issue; the men's request that their colleagues be re-instated was rejected so the miners walked out bringing the entire colliery to a standstill.

Richard Fosdick did not stand idle, he informed the press:

'He would commence legal proceedings against his workers.'

The dispute was settled the following week with Fosdick agreeing to pay 1 penny per ton in advance on some kinds of work. At this time the *'best coal from the pit was being sold in London for 6/- per ton'*.

In spite of his quick recourse to law Richard Fosdick, at least in the early period running his Colliery, appears to have been a progressive voice among the coal owners and popular with his employees; the main reason for this popularity may have been based on the fact:

'He had opposed a general reduction of wages last December and had argued in the newspaper that it was of no advantage to the coal owners to do this.'

As the overall economic conditions of the Country deteriorated the Fitzwilliam Hemsworth Colliery Company felt the impact. By the 5th of July 1879 the pit was closed because of the depressed state of the coal market and the financial straits of the company. A petition for the liquidation of the affairs of M.G.A. Fosdick, Coal Proprietor and Coal Merchant of Hemsworth and Cambridge Rd, St Pancras, London, was filed in July of the same year. Debts were returned at £100,000, and assets, apart from the Fitzwilliam Hemsworth Colliery Company, at £1,400.

The Wakefield Express of the 12th of July claimed it was:

'The largest failure which has taken place in South Yorkshire.'

The company's creditors wasted no time in trying to recover some of the company's assets. On the 23rd some of them tried to remove a locomotive engine from the pit head. Mr Bennet, the colliery manager, prevented them by having colliers remove the rail track joining the pit to the Great Northern Railways Line. With nowhere to go, the locomotive remained on-site.

'The formal meeting of the creditors held on Wednesday 30th at the Great Northern Hotel, Leeds, identified unsecured liabilities of some £16,670 and assets estimated at £9,760, it was accepted that it was somewhat doubtful if a large portion of these will ever be realised.'

The Landlord had taken possession of the colliery and continued to pay workers to keep the pumps running. By August the 9th he refused to continue this and stopped the pumps allowing 25,000 gallons of water per hour to flow into the pit workings.

Mr Close, a Leeds based accountant, was appointed as Trustee of Fosdick's estate and quickly assumed control. At Leeds Bankruptcy court on Wednesday the 13th of August Vincent Thompson, on behalf of the trustee, applied for a disclaimer on the lease of the colliery. This lease was dated 1st August 1877 and was for a term of 42 years. The application was made because for some time the colliery had been unworkable at a profit due to faults in the strata. Mr Beverly, appearing for the property owner, the *Right Honourable Charles Fitzwilliam*, did not object to the disclaimer. Mr West, representing the mortgagers of very substantial sums of money, asked that it should not be prejudicial to the rights of his clients. The action was successful and a ruling given that:

'The trustee would be allowed to disclaim without prejudice to the mortgaged securities.'

On Monday the 18th of August on the instruction of Mr Close, the personal and domestic possessions of Richard Fosdick's Hemsworth residence, Acacia Cottage, along with plant and machinery from the brickyard and colliery, were auctioned off.

In an effort to save the intrinsic value of the pits Mr Close had the pumps draining water from the colliery workings re-started before the end of that month. This action did little to reassure many of the colliers who had moved to the area. Indeed the uncertainty over the colliery's future motivated a substantial number of them to seek work elsewhere. This can be seen from the fact that in the collier's houses in Kinsley only 1 of the 30 houses in Jackson Terrace was occupied, likewise out of 34 houses in Fitzwilliam Terrace 18 were vacant.

Not all of the town's population felt this despair. In a few areas of Hemsworth the forces of prosperity and progress were displayed; with The Wakefield Express proudly announcing:

'We notice that Mr W H. Leatham of Hemsworth Hall has, at his sole expense fixed about a dozen public lamps in various parts of the village and this generous act on his part has proved a great boon to the villagers. At present there is no supply of gas in the district, and the lamps are supplied with paraffin oil, but they have been so constructed and fixed, that when gas is introduced into the locality – and it is much needed – the lamps can be utilised.

They are lighted (sic) every evening at dusk by William Scholey, the sexton of the church, and the same person acts as light trimmer and also extinguisher of the lights about eleven o'clock at night. Mr Richard Fosdick colliery proprietor has also fixed a lamp in front of his residence and Mr Leatham's example is also being followed by some of the other principal residents of this pleasant and rapidly growing district.'

Work at the colliery re-started around the end of August.

On Saturday morning in early September the village was rocked by a large explosion from the colliery. Five men were killed as a result of a gas explosion. Two of the men were killed instantly, the other three lived for between 12 and 24 hours after the event, before dying from head injuries and burns. The dead men were:

'George Hill.	*44.*	*Coal Getter.*	*Bracken Hill.*
John Mann.	*25/26.*	*Coal Getter.*	*Bracken Hill.*
John Wm Rushton.	*36.*	*Coal Getter.*	*Bracken Hill.*
Isaiah James.	*33.*	*Coal Getter.*	*Fitzwilliam. Tce.*
Paul Brailsford.	*32.*	*Coal Getter.*	*Crofton.'*

An enquiry headed by a Captain Taylor and assisted by the Government Inspector of Mines, as well as Fosdick, Bennet, Millar and Ben Pickard, Secretary of the Miners Association, was set up to examine the cause. Benjamin Cope, day deputy of Fitzwilliam Terrace, gave an account of events leading up to and following the explosion:

'I went down about six o'clock on Saturday morning saw Bird and took his report. We talked together for ten minutes or so. All was

satisfactory as far as I know, except that a fall of stone had taken place, but nothing, which could have affected those people who were killed. About half past six the men started to come down. They all work with candles. Rushton left word that he would want a shot firing, but when I went to him about half past seven, he said he thought he could do without it.

The men do not fire their own shots, I am the shot firer. Rushton had not drilled a hole but was cutting the coal down instead. He was at the gate end next to the face. Everything was apparently in good order. I then went to Green's and James's place but at that time they were doing nothing, and their place was apparently all right as was also the place of two men named Wright and Brown. Getting to Hill's and Mann's place I found a shot ready for firing and I fired it. This was about a quarter to eight. I don't remember that they had left a message about wanting a shot firing.

Beyond the firing of the shot I heard nothing. The roof was all right: I heard no weighting and no one had made any complaint.

Nearly ten o'clock, when at the north end I was fetched by George Brown and went to the west board and saw Mann and Hill laid down on the board opposite the gate end where they worked. They were crying out for help. I got them put in a corf and taken out. Rushton was lying dead in the same place.

I tried to go along Hill's gate but was stopped by a fall from the roof. I then tried Green's gate and found a fall of stone there. Going through a slit a little higher up, where a stopping had been blown out, I found Isaiah James in a sitting posture and he asked me to lay him down. I held him in my arms till others came to remove him. I had not noticed any smell till I reached the top of the west board, when I smelt (sic) after-damp very strongly, accompanied with a little smoke. An hour and a half elapsed before the smoke and stench were cleared away. Mr William Fulwood who occupied a farm nearby very kindly granted the use of his carts and horses to remove the injured men to their homes and he also sent a quantity of bedding.'

The coroner's summation gave a clear direction to the jury:

'The evidence did not throw much light on the cause of the explosion by which these men were killed. One thing however was certain, that the pit was considered so very clear of gas that candles were used and that not the slightest suspicion of an explosion had entered the minds of anybody.'

After a short consultation the jury returned their verdict:

'We consider the death of these men was purely accidental and that no one was to blame; at the same time we think Mr Fosdick has adopted a very proper course in introducing safety lamps.'

Not everyone reached the same conclusion, one local journalist was of the opinion that:

'Though the immediate cause of the mishap was not easily ascertainable it is supposed that a fall of coal must have liberated sufficient gas to ignite on coming into contact with the uncovered flame of the candles... ...Had safety lamps been in use there is very little doubt that there would have been no explosion, for it is evident that the quantity of gas that ignited as well as any accumulations could not have been very large, otherwise the damage would have been much greater. The explosion however furnishes another illustration of the danger incurred in working any of the seams of coal in South Yorkshire with naked lights.'

From our viewpoint there is little value in trying to apportion blame, however it is noted that soon after this incident Mr Bennet, the Colliery Manager, moved to nearby Stanley Colliery.

During the next few years Fosdick struggled to keep his colliery, now registered as the *Hemsworth Colliery Company Ltd*, going as a commercial entity. The business appears to have been run by liquidators from around 1886 until the formation of *The New Hemsworth Colliery Company Ltd* in 1898.

This was a vehicle set up by Fosdick with support from the Manchester business community to lease and work the pit. Within a short space of time the place was buzzing with activity. John Higson of Manchester was appointed Colliery Engineer and immediately tried to solve the problem of water flooding the workings. A new set of big water-pumps were ordered and fitted and two new cages for carrying miners to the bottom of the pit, with tanks at the bottom of each for drawing water as well as coal, were made at the Railway Foundry, Barnsley, and fitted to the winding gear.

During these weeks the village also became a hive of activity with construction workers as well as large numbers of ponies carrying vast quantities of stores, arriving daily.

As the pit was being re-built the township of Hemsworth grew significantly and the population swelled to approximately 5,200 persons. This expansion motivated the Barnsley Co-op Society to open a store in Hemsworth. The new Co-op was a fine addition to the town, costing £2,600, it was built using Brighouse and Huddersfield stone and provided a grocers', butchers, drapers, boot and shoe department, plus a milliners and dressmaking showroom. To celebrate the opening the Co-op invited around 300 townspeople to a party in the local church hall.

In Kinsley the miner's housing now comprised six rows of terraced dwellings providing around 136 houses; to educate the miner's children a school was in the process of being built in the village. This was a much smaller project than the Co-op building, costing a mere £997-8s-0d, the site itself costing £200.

With these developments the colliery became the major employer in the area, over 2000 men and boys now working three seams of coal, namely the Barnsley Bed, the Shafton Seam and the Haigh Moor.

Unfortunately for the new company and its employees the good times were short lived. In a valiant effort to keep the pit working as a viable entity Richard Fosdick appeared to wheel and deal with a series of backers and bankers from London and Doncaster as well as with Percy Tew of Heath Hall, Wakefield. However the last quarter of the 19th and beginning of the 20th centuries were characterised by economic depression and widespread industrial unrest. A glimpse of this can be seen from the fact that during the National Strike of July the 28th 1893 some 277,000 men and boys stopped work in an attempt to dissuade the owners from forcing a 25% cut in wages.

Although the macro economic factors were extremely significant in both their cause and effect on employment in Hemsworth, I choose not to deal with these wider social and economic issues here, mainly because these events have been covered in detail by others.

Brief Summary

The James Report and its Effects

As deteriorating economic conditions constrained the National Economy they devastated the market for coal and of course profits of the Colliery Owners. In an effort to find a solution to the problem the government set up an enquiry, headed by *Lord James,* to examine the issues affecting the collieries and make recommendations to alleviate the industry's problems.

The report of this enquiry, known as *The James Report*, was given in August 1903. Its publication had a profound and almost immediate effect on the industry. In essence the report recommended a 5% reduction in miner's wages; Colliery Owners seized upon this idea and implemented a 5% wage cut before the end of that month.

The industrial unrest that followed the Colliery Owners action was nation-wide. A few extracts from newspapers of the time are included to convey the sense of outrage at the wage cut:

'The Scottish Miners Federation who instructed their delegates to the National Conference of Miners in Stockport on Saturday 3rd September to vote for a stoppage of work over the entire British

Miners Federation area in the event of the Scotch (sic) Coal Masters on September 7th reducing the present minimum wage of 3/6d per day.'

A meeting of the representatives of South Wales and Monmouthshire miners held in Cardiff:

'Resolved to support the Scotch (sic) miners in maintaining the minimum rate of wages.'

Within the ridings of Yorkshire reaction to the Report was speedy but uncoordinated and patchy:

'On Wednesday 31st August a deputation of Enginemen employed at Altofts by Messrs Pope and Pearson' s West Riding Collieries waited upon the managing director Mr W. E. Garforth. The deputation was duly informed that as a consequence of the Master's Association the reduction would have to come off.'

'Pits at Park Hill of the Victoria Coal Company ceased working at the end of August /beginning of September.'

On Thursday the 1st of September some of the Castleford boys employed by Henry Briggs and Sons refused to work, as a consequence the pit was *Flushed* half a day. At Wheldale Colliery miners came out on a one-day strike. Likewise a strike by 200 boys stopped 1000 men working at Wynstay Colliery. At Middleton Colliery Leeds management: *'overcame idleness of 700 men and boys by employing new enginemen.'*

On Friday the 2nd of September:

'Management claim the reduction of 3d per day is due to depression in the coal trade.'

It should be noted however that miner's reactions to these cuts varied throughout the Ridings of Yorkshire.

The James report specifically examined the problems associated with participants in the coal industry's Joint Conciliation Boards and his findings relevant to these parties; however the Colliery Owners applied the 5% cut to every area of work within their control. Colliery Enginemen, who were not members of the Joint Conciliation Board, found their wages being cut by the same amount as the miners. Given that the number of enginemen employed at each pit was insignificant, augmented by the fact that the average wage for an engineman was between 35 shillings and 2 guineas per week, the savings made at each pit by reducing enginemen's wages would not have been substantial. Indeed some workers suggested the *Masters* had a hidden agenda, as one engineman remarked to his local newspaper:

'This situation is created by the masters, not because they covet the infinitesimal economy that would be effected, but for the purpose of finding an excuse for shutting down the pits whilst the heavy stocks on hand are got rid of, i.e. it is a case of either reducing the stocks in hand or reducing the price of coal.'

Some credence for this view is given by the *East West Yorkshire Union Railways Report of 1904* which identifies the:

'Total weight of goods and mineral traffic over railway for the
½ year up to 30th June 1904 was 426,538 tons.
½ " " " " " 1903 " 478,187 tons.'

The Railway Company's analysis identified:

'The fall off in net revenue from £6,246 to £2,974 was due to a heavy decrease in mineral traffic.'

At the beginning of September the Enginemen's Society issued a circular giving their views on the 5% reduction of wages. Their argument was, they were not connected with the Conciliation Board therefore they were not bound by Lord James's recommendations.

They asked that no reduction be made on their member's wages pending a meeting with the South and West Yorkshire Coal Owners Association to discuss the question and try to establish machinery for governing variations in surface worker's wages.

At the National Executive meeting in February 1904 The National Federation of Colliery Enginemen's Association passed the following resolution:

'The committee would gladly welcome any arrangement that would provide for the regulation of Colliery Enginemen's and Boilermen's wages by the present conciliation board, if they could have proper representation on that board and a satisfactory basic fixed. Seeing that Colliery Enginemen and other Enginemen's and Boilermen's wages have not been advanced with the miner's wages, we consider that any attempted reduction in consequence of Lord James's decision should be resisted.'

The Labour Gazette of September detailed the effect of the wage cuts during this period:

'The changes in rates of wages reported during August affected nearly 367,000 work people, of whom only about 900 received advances, whilst 365,700 maintained decreases, the latter chiefly affecting coal miners in the Federated Districts of England and in South Yorkshire, South Staffordshire and East Worcester. The net effect of all the changes was a decrease of over £17,600.0.0d per week.'

Chapter Two

Storm Clouds Gathering

The Hemsworth Colliery worked on day wages until June 1900 at a rate of 1 shilling and 4 pence per ton, with miners guaranteed a wage of 7 shillings and 3 pence per day. In March 1901 the colliery stopped paying miners working the Barnsley Seam at this wage rate, a six month strike by workers in this seam ensued. The strike ended when a new arrangement of 2 shillings and 2 pence per ton was agreed and implemented for a trial period of 18 months, i.e. until the 31st of March 1903.

In an attempt to eliminate wage conflict a clause in the settlement stated that three months before the termination date of the agreement talks would be held between Fosdick, the Y.M.A. and delegates from the local union branch. In the event of these talks failing to agree on terms and conditions the matter would automatically go to arbitration. The Arbitrator appointed by the Joint Board would make recommendations that were final and binding on both parties. In spite of this clause imposing compulsory arbitration, wage disputes continued and resulted in four hundred men being dismissed on the

10th of August due to a stoppage of work. In an attempt to resolve the dispute, Charles Atkinson, Stipendiary Magistrate for the City of Leeds, was appointed to act as *Arbitrator* between the colliery and the miners. The terms of reference for Mr Atkinson's investigation were, he:

'Should have power to order and determine what should be done by either of the parties respecting the matters in difference' and that his: *'Award should be final and binding upon the Company and upon the Miners employed in working the said seam.'*

Willing to await the Arbiter's decision, miners in the Barnsley seam returned to work.

On the 23rd of September 1903 the Umpire's decision was announced. The miners were awarded 1 shilling 11½ pence per ton as the getting price for coal in this seam. Two days after the award was announced, James Crerar, Secretary of the Colliery Company, sent a telegram to Ben Pickard, miners M.P. and Y.M.A. President. This was followed by a letter, sent on September the 30th, which informed the miner's leaders the company could not honour the commitment and pay the wage rates recommended by the Atkinson report:

'Dear Sir
Referring to our telegram of September 25th, and your reply thereto of the same date, we have as you are aware taken up this award, which we have most anxiously considered.

We feel sure that you will agree with us that it quite impossible for us to compete with our neighbours under the unfavourable conditions of the Award seeing that at South Kirkby, Sharlston, Monckton, Acton Hall and Featherstone, the getting prices are as much as 1s per ton below the award for these Collieries.'

Mr Currer's letter did not change the position of the miners or their leaders. They believed the Arbitrator had heard the arguments from both sides and had reached an objective decision. The company however maintained its position and called a meeting with a deputation of miners from the Barnsley seam to discuss the position. During this meeting delegates were told the company had decided the *Getting Price* given by the arbitrator was too high. As a consequence the colliery manager advised delegates the awarded price list would be further revised downwards. The colliers refused to accept the revised offer, insisting on the fact that:

'The arbitration award was binding on both parties.'

The Colliery Company responded by issuing notices of *Termination of Employment* to the entire workforce employed on the Barnsley seam. Industrial relations were worsened by the company's proposal to reduce its enginemen's wages by 3 pence. When the enginemen rejected the company's proposal they were issued with a *Notice of Termination* of employment. New enginemen were hired to replace those sacked, however the men's inexperience of this type of work caused serious safety problems.

On Sunday the 11th of September as the nightshift was due to begin in the Shafton Seam:

'A cage full of miners went down but for some reason when the bottom was reached the cage went with a smash......injuring several men, ... surgical aid was required for some. As a result other men refused to go down stating that the enginemen were incompetent.'

On Monday the 12th miners working the Shafton seam refused to go down arguing that the winders were incompetent. Some did work on Tuesday and an increasing number worked on Wednesday and Thursday, however the majority would not work because they felt:

'Under prevailing conditions it was too dangerous to do so.'

The Haigh Moor seam *played* for want of enginemen until Thursday morning when the men were told the pit would be worked and that new enginemen had been hired, unfortunately:

'They Pulled twice during the morning and the men had to be got out by some other means.'

On Friday evening September the 16th feeling was so strong that Mr Harper was asked by a deputation of miners to withdraw the enginemen at one of the shafts, (this was probably the Shafton seam), on the grounds that they were in great danger. Mr Harper at once paid the engineman off and directed another man to take his place. The winding continued to be unsatisfactory to the miners so a deputation again visited the manager and asked him to withdraw the new winders and re-instate the old hands. Mr Harper '*absolutely refused.*'

Having no success in their negotiations with the company the local miner's branch referred the issue to the Government Inspector of Mines, the Yorkshire Miners Association and Mr Pickard of the Y.M.A. As well as informing the parties mentioned previously they also telegraphed Mr Fosdick, the Managing Director of the Colliery Company, asking him to meet them to discuss the issue; Fosdick declined this invitation claiming he did not interfere with Mr Harper's decisions. It is interesting to note the formalisation of the devolution of power from colliery owner to the manager, a feature that became commonplace as industries matured:

'*Workers faced with a dispute or disagreement with the manager could no longer call at the owner's house and try to resolve the issue with him. The Colliers now had to deal with a manager whose authority was severely constrained by the owner.*'

This process was described by Phelps–Brown as one in which:

'Remote power became more common and workers had to deal with a poker faced man whose relation with you was dehumanised and straight jacketed.'

The position of workers in general and colliers in particular was severely limited by the introduction of a legislative framework which increasingly governed actions in this area. New Industrial Relations Laws outlawed spontaneous action by local branches. This was highlighted by one local newspaper reporter of the time who explained to his readers:

'Local Miners Leaders found themselves in a very unpleasant position as owing to the uncertainty of the liability of Trade Unions under certain circumstances, a condition brought about by the Taff Vale and Denaby Main decisions,... they do not feel justified, even if danger were proved, in advising the men to stay away from the pits.'

The Taff Vale and Denaby Main cases brought chaos to union branches. The effect of these decisions on the Hemsworth miners was described by the Wakefield Express as follows:

'Whatever the merits of the case, the men are without leaders, each acts on his own responsibility with the inevitable result that some of the men were working, others were not, what the outcome will be no one can foresee, much will depend upon what the Government Inspector says and the nature of the advice the officials of the Miners Association of Barnsley may be able to offer. In the meantime a decidedly unpleasant state of affairs exists.'

The despondency in the Hemsworth/Kinsley mining community created by this new legislative framework was compounded by the anger caused by inaccurate reports of their case in some national newspapers:

'A number of men are angry at reports in some of the daily newspapers this week, to the effect that they had met and passed a resolution to set down the collieries. This is not correct as positively no aggregate meeting of the men had been held up to the time the report in question appeared.'

The men's withdrawal of labour brought about by the company's use of inexperienced enginemen continued to cause problems at the Shafton seam. It is difficult to ascertain exactly how many men and boys refused to go down the pit. All one can say with confidence is that a majority refused to do so.

For those miners who did return to work hostility between the pit manager and the working miners continued unabated. Matters between the parties were brought to a head on Saturday the 24th of September when 26 miners and pony drivers working in the *Old Pit* were summoned to appear at Pontefract court for breaches of bye laws.

It became clear that boys had refused to follow the manager's instructions to drive ponies in areas where there was up to 1 foot of water on the ground. The court dismissed these actions because they should have been brought under the special rules for damages for breach of contract, not for breach of bye-laws which were not recognised in law. The colliery's lawyer immediately had fresh summons issued, this time under the proper legislation. The men's representative responded by stating:

'If the manager does not cease his arbitrary behaviour towards the employees of the Hemsworth Colliery, there will never be any chance of working amicably together.'

It is important to remember, in communities dependent on a single industry the effects of short time working, strikes or lock-outs were, and indeed still are, quickly transmitted to almost every part of the local economy; in the Township of Hemsworth by the end of September:

'All over the district the trades people are bitterly complaining of the serious depression and are hoping for a speedy settlement.'

A modicum of relief for those miners injured in the earlier accidents in the pit cages was given by the news:

'Miners officials report that men who were Pulled some time ago are in serious condition. The company are paying compensation; officials are sorry this is necessary and that these men have to suffer so much through someone else's fault.'

On Saturday the 15th of October over £1,000 union money was paid out to over 1200 men for the time they *Played* through the *Pulling* accidents in the Haigh Moor and Shafton Seams.

By the end of the second week of October 1904 the water problems plaguing the Shafton Seam were much worse, the men who continued to work there had been sent home every day due to the breakthrough of water. The already bad situation was made worse by recriminations between miners working this seam and the colliery manager. On the one side the colliers argued the break-in of water was due to bad management, the manager replying it was merely bad luck. During the third week of October the Colliery Company tried to restore a degree of normality by posting notices informing miners:

'Both seams were now working normally and that if any man plays two days in any week he will be given notice or otherwise dealt with.'

During the following week a breakdown of the pumping engines caused water levels to rise in the Haigh Moor seam binging work to a halt. As if these problems were not enough for the company to handle, work in the Shafton seam was halted when strands of the cage rope began to break. The Inspector of Mines was sent for and the rope duly condemned, causing the whole of the pit to stand idle. A new rope was ordered and arrived at the pithead during the week ending the 12th of November; unfortunately the new rope was too short. A new pulley rope was ordered and fitted by the 19th allowing work to be re-started. Although this major problem had been solved the constant ingress of water continued to be a problem for workers in this seam.

In an attempt to maximise sales in the difficult marketplace, colliery managers implemented a three month trial recovering and selling the cheaper *Top Coal* instead of the *Bed Coal.* This decision caused some concern among the miners who complained bitterly because they:

'Cannot see reasoning behind management asking them to take out Top Coal, by doing so the Top Coal had to be propped up which required more timbering. The men claimed the company was acting irrationally insofar as they could not sell the other coal yet they are digging out Top Coal which pays 2/1d per ton less than Bed Coal.

I assume that the recovery of the *top coal* was an attempt by the company to test the viability of selling lower-priced, lower grade coal in the depressed domestic coal market with a view to recovering the remaining coals when the demand for steam coal improved. By so doing the manager would also hope to extend the life of the Shafton Seam.

The experiment of digging out the *top coal* got off to a bad start; *James Atack* was badly hurt on Tuesday the 22nd and *John Whole* of Ackworth was killed on the morning of the 24th of November whilst working under the trial system.

Feeling among the men continued to run high, the majority of miners now thinking it was time to bring all work at the Hemsworth Colliery to a halt:

'It is said that the men have asked permission to ballot the whole of the workers as to whether all the pits should stand until all the grievances have been settled. On the other hand, it is said that the Barnsley seam will be restarted as soon as the coke ovens, now being erected, have been finished.'

At the Yorkshire Miners Association Council meeting in Barnsley the week ending the 12th of November, it was decided to ask the district to ballot as to whether the workers on the other two seams should come out on strike over the grievances, and so set down the whole of the colliery. The result would be declared at the next ordinary meeting of the Y. M.A. council.

It is important to remember that colliers working the Barnsley seam had now been *locked out* for some 12 weeks. *Nipsey Money* (that is monies collected through donations), was added to each mans strike pay which meant nearly 500 men received 1 shilling or 2 shillings a week on top of the Y.M.A. strike pay to help feed themselves and their families.

To raise funds for this cause concerts were given in Hemsworth Council Schools on Monday and Tuesday the 14th and 15th of November. Mr T. Walton provided the talent free in a programme comprising:

'Cinematograph Views of the Euro-Jap War, and artistes, Professor Woodhead, the sisters Gordon, Miss Willows and Fred Walton.' Mr W Lincoln presiding *'asked for all present to rally behind the miners seeing Christmas was approaching. His appeal met with a hearty response with a total profit of £10.0.0 being made, £5 of which went to the miners.'*

Additional assistance was given to the families when in December the Halifax Flour Company donated 40 stones of flour; a similar donation was made the following week by the Wakefield Industrial Society.

For Christmas the Yorkshire Miners Association doubled its strike pay to 13 shillings per man plus 2 shillings for each child in the family. In the true spirit of mining communities those miners remaining in work contributed coal and food to their less fortunate neighbours and colleagues.

On the 7th of January miner's officials accompanied by a deputation of colliers agreed to meet the colliery manager to explore the possibility of finding a solution to the grievances. It appears to have been generally accepted by the mining community that if no agreement could be found the colliers would be balloted on the question of:

'The whole of the pits coming out.'

By the 14th of January 1905 things were fairly bleak, no *Nipsey Money* was paid out and

'A number of men who live in Colliery Houses at Kinsley have received notices to quit.'

From our perspective in time it is difficult to imagine the conditions facing the miners and their families as they waited to be thrown out of their homes. It must have felt that everything, including the weather was against them, as winter brought temperatures so low:

'Work at the quarries in Ackworth was stopped for on Monday and Tuesday. Several of the older employees described it as the worst they had seen for 20 years with frost penetrating the stone to a depth of one foot making boring operations almost impossible.'

In a further attempt to resolve the Hemsworth miner's grievances officials of the Yorkshire Miners Association met with the Colliery Directors in Leeds. Mr Fosdick, Managing Director of the colliery '*promised that he would do his best to put things right.*' Nothing came of this, indeed according to one newspaper the situation became even more complex, the:

'Biggest grievance is the dirt question. The company (so we are informed) is persisting in giving men notice for having dirt among the coal and practically ignoring the Check Weigh Act which says that the checkweighman and the man appointed by the company shall deal with the coal dirt and reductions can be made. This, the company refuse to allow giving men notice instead.'

In the same week voting on the *Ballot* in the two pits to determine '*whether all the pits should be put down'* had taken place. The results were:

'Haigh Moor.	*In favour of coming out.*	*306*
	Against coming out.	*91*
Shafton.	*In favour of coming out.*	*203*
	Against coming out.	*202*

2 spoilt votes and 1 blank paper

The Haigh Moor result is in accordance with the Rules of the Y.M.A. but the Shafton Ballot was not; the necessary majority not being obtained for the giving in of notice. The matter will be decided upon at Monday's meeting of the Yorkshire Council at Barnsley.'

By the 28th of January miner's officials were seeking provision to hold a fresh ballot at both Haigh Moor and Shafton seams because:

'Proper facilities were not given to the men to record their votes as the pits played on the day when the ballot should have been taken.'

In the same week a local reporter claimed to have been informed:

'That approximately 30 mechanics etc, working at the top have been given notice. It is also alleged that there is to be a reduction in wages all round.'

By the end of the second week of February *Nipsey Money* was reduced to one shilling. For the families of the locked-out miners living in Ackworth additional assistance was received through the donation of 400 loaves by Pontefract Co-op. Whilst it seemed obvious the Hemsworth miners were struggling to feed their families, local newspapers of the period indicated:

'*The majority of support in Yorkshire is going to the miners of Corton Wood Colliery who are out and receiving no money from the Yorkshire Miners Association.*'

At the national level, the Conference of the *Miners Federation of Great Britain* voted to send a deputation of its members to the Chancellor of the Exchequer asking him to consider abolishing the Coal Tax. The collier's delegation was followed a few days later, on the 25th February, by a deputation of *Coalowners, Exporters and Shippers of the United Kingdom* urging the removal of tax on exported coal. The Chancellor:

'*Mr Austin Chamberlain in reply said he could not make his budget statement in snippets. He had received the deputation in order to hear their views but he was unable to give them any indication of his state of mind or of his purpose in connexion with the coming budget.*'

In a further attempt at resolution John Higson, mining engineer at the colliery, wrote to the Y.M.A officials asking them to meet a deputation at the Great Northern hotel, Leeds:

'*To try if a new price list can be arranged for the Barnsley Bed. At a substantial reduction and also a reduction in the tonnage rate, ripping etc at the Haigh Moor pit. If no arrangement is arrived at the whole of the works will have to be set down.*'

In Hemsworth miners met to discuss the letter and select a deputation to represent them. Whilst waiting for the meeting with the colliery manager to take place, their patience was further strained when on Saturday the 25th of March the:

'Chairman of Pontefract West Riding Bench Mr B. Lowden was engaged for over 4 hours on Saturday hearing summonses against 20 miners employed at the Hemsworth Fitzwilliam Colliery.'

The men had been charged with *'having unlawfully absented themselves from work',* and against which claims for damages were sought by the Company.

Mr Chas Lowden, solicitor, prosecuted, Mr Willey, solicitor, represented the defendants. Evidence for the prosecution was given in almost every case by the under manager; most of the defendants gave evidence on their own behalf.

The company's claim which dated from March the 6th, was based on the assertion that no sufficient reason had been given for the men's absence from work. The prosecuting solicitor claimed:

'At the colliery now there was not only a Collier Monday but a Treat Thursday. Indeed the men seem to think that they should not be debarred from taking a holiday when they choose. Some of the defendants had absented themselves for one day, some two days, some for three days.

In the Shafton seam alone 349 individual shifts were lost per week meaning that 1200 tons of coal that should have been raised were not raised. The Colliery Company were not acting at all capriciously in the matter, but felt that some stand had to be made. They were entitled to the services of the defendants daily by agreement.'

First Witness: Mr Francis Elliot, under-manager in Haigh Moor Seam, speaking on the case of Mr Hodgekin who was absent from work on the 6th of March claimed:

"The reason as stated by the defendant was that he was playing a dart match at which he won £11.0.0. "He added" *if he had the chance he would take another holiday. The firm would lose 3 tons*

of coal by the defendant's actions and working costs would be increased. 7/- was a fair amount to claim per day."

Mr Willey: Strongly urged that "*supposing the company lost the raising of 3 tons of coal, they didn't lose anything appreciable thereby, and if they did it had nothing to do with the damages claimed."*

Magistrates Clerk: (Mr Leatham) "*I am of the opinion it did."*

Mr Willey: "*An arrangement between men and Mr Harper was reached under which the company agreed the men might absent themselves one or two days a week."*

Clerk: "*The men have contracted to work 6 days a week."*

Chairman: "*If you can show there was an agreement we shall have no more to say."*

Mr Lowden: "*We are proceeding on a written contract any other agreement must also be in writing."*

Chairman: "*Yes we must have it in writing."*

Mr Willey: "*I shall prove that it was put up at the pit."*

Mr Harper: (manager) was then sworn in and started speaking on the damages claimed:

"*Seven shillings was much below the actual cost. The standing charge amounted to over four shillings – per ton.* "The witness denied" *there had been any arrangement that the men might 'play' one day a week. He did put up a notice that the men absenting themselves would be dismissed."*

On cross-examination: "*he did not dismiss any one after the notices but warned some.*

The pit was not working that day and (March 8th) *and were not paying anyone 7/- per day."*

Likewise, *"he did not remember any conference about the men having a 'play' day per week."*

First Defendant: *"He had never broken any time from his own fault and had never had a complaint laid against him. He had complained of the heat of the working place to Mr Wallace and of the need for ventilation. He was sick as a consequence of the heat. He did play a darts match in the evening but this did not keep him away from work. He had worked 5 days a week for the past month."*

The next case, charged with being absent on March the 6th.

Wilkinson Riley: "*Was away from home and did not get back in time to go to work.*"

Prosecutor: *"The man was a habitual absentee."*

Riley: "*Went to see his sick mother in Drighlington and did not get back to Tuesday.*"

Prosecutor: "*The man was a habitual absentee.*"

Next charged was **William Varley:** who had "*overlaid himself*".

Mr Varley had "*walked 10 miles a day to his work and back, 5 miles each way and could not get a house any nearer. He had to get up at 3.30 in the morning and reached home about 4.30pm. He had often walked to the colliery and back and been told there was no work. He had done that 3 days in one week.*"

Alfred Terry: "*laid too long*" admitted this and said "*no complaint had ever been made of his absence previously.*"

William Rimmington: absent on March the 6th and 9th. The amount of 14 shillings was being claimed from him. In his defence Mr Rimmington stated: "*Many a time he had to return from the pit when there was no work and he had been kept in the pit for two hours in his wet clothes.*"

William Weathrall's case was adjourned as he was at that time suffering from an injury he had sustained at work.

Henry Nicholson: Was described as a man who did not attend regularly. He had not been asked for his reason. He had "*worked for the company for 22 years. He was absent on the occasion complained of because he was not well from a bad cold. He contended that he had a right to absent himself one day out of six.*"

George Palmer: Was absent through a slight accident which was not reported until after the summons was issued: "*He tried to work and the doctor afterwards told him he should not have gone to work with a back like that.*"

On cross-examination he agreed: "*He did not get a doctors certificate until after the summons was issued.*"

John Mills: Described by the prosecutor as a "*very bad one for playing.*" Mr Willey the defending solicitor had not been instructed in this case. Consequently an order was made against him.

John Hall: No reason given for his absence: "*He had never broken a minute during the 6 months he had been employed at the pit. He had often been sent back from no fault of his. Was only absent because of an injured finger. The deputy saw the injury. He had come out twice in one week from want of timber.*"

Mr Lowden: (prosecutor) withdrew the summons against this defendant.

James Hall: "*Could not go to work not being a qualified miner, because of the enforced absence of his brother.*" James Hall drew some laughter from the courtroom as he stated: "*His check had been stopped only once and he had 7½ days to draw that very week.*"

Enoch Caswell: Had worked for the colliery for 4 years, he had not given a reason for his absence: *"He was absent from influenza and a medical certificate produced. He claimed he had lost 3 days wages when work was not to be had.*"

Frank Gordon: No reason for his absence was given. The company claimed: *"He was one of the worst offenders.*" The reason now being given for his absence was oversleeping.

Sam Shelton: Absent on March the 6th, he had been absent for 1 day during the month: *"The deputy knew he was subject to attacks of acute rheumatism, he could not walk on the 6th.*"

Thomas Gibson: It was found that he had suffered an accident to his *Breast* (sic) on March 3rd whilst at work. This summons was then withdrawn.

Peter Hines: "*Had suffered from diarrhoea as shown by his doctor's certificate. When he found he was likely to Play On he got a certificate and sent it to the office,*" (dated the 9th), after being summoned he got another certificate dated the 6th.

George Fish: Absent on March the 9th and 10th. Mr Fish had presented himself for work but refused to so do as: "*The place was a victim place*", he re-iterated that, *"he did not refuse to work except in a certain place."*

MrWilley: (defendants solicitor) *"Refused to an order in this case of 14/-." (sic).*

Sam Wild and R. E. Hewitt: Were the other defendants; both had refused to work along with Fish.

In the case of **George Walsh:** The company was claiming 21 shillings for 3 days absence and Mr Walsh had submitted a counter claim against the colliery. Mr Walsh had refused to move dirt prior to entering upon his day's work. On another day he was sent back, whilst on one more day he could not work because of want of timber, hence his counter claim.

The ordinary evidence having been concluded:

Mr Willey: then went on to show that an arrangement was made on the 20th of May last: "*By which the men were permitted to absent themselves one day a week eventually two if they thought fit.*"

Edgar Cuthbert: Deposed that, on Mr Harper's suggestion:

"*It was agreed that if a man worked 5 days it would be satisfactory and occasionally he could work only 4 and on the strength of this arrangement a notice was fixed on the pithead.*"

Edgar Cuthbert's deposition was fully supported by other witnesses including John Potts, plus Messrs Goddard, Garbutt and Watmough.

After a brief recess the court accepted the notice (produced from the pithead) was an indication the men might play one day a week. Consequently damages were only awarded to the company in cases where the defendant had been absent from work for two or more days in the same week. Rimmington and Fish had therefore to pay 7 shillings each, Hewitt had to pay in respect of 2 days. All the other summonses were dismissed and costs awarded.

The Hemsworth Colliery Company was not alone in using the legal system to discipline its employees. Indeed a perspective on how employees were viewed by other employers can be gained from the following article printed in the Hemsworth Express of the period:

The *'South Kirkby Coal Company took 15 pony drivers to court at Pontefract at the beginning of April. The pony drivers were charged with having left work without giving proper notice.'*

The accused had left work because another lad had been dismissed. Mr Clayton-Smith (prosecutor) in claiming 3 shillings from the defendants asserted: *'cases could not be looked at complacently. He hoped they would receive a lesson that day which would teach them not to disrespect the authority of their superiors.'*

The court duly found in favour of the colliery awarding 3 shillings damages plus costs against all of the lads accused.

In The Court of Appeal the following month the arguments were concluded in the landmark case between The Denaby and Cadeby Main Collieries Ltd Vs Yorkshire Miners Association and others, in which the defendants moved for a judgement or a new trial. The Plaintiffs, (Denaby and Cadeby Main Collieries Ltd), brought the action to recover £140,000 in damages for an *Unlawful Conspiracy* by the Y.M.A. in trying to induce the company's workers to take strike action.

In the lower court a verdict had been given in favour of the Colliery Company but the award of damages *Stood Over* pending an appeal, on this occasion their Lordships reserved judgement.

Whilst the Y.M.A. contested these cases in the courts circumstances in Hemsworth worsened. At the beginning of April a grant of £15 had been made to the locked out miners from Wales. This enabled the paying of families around two shillings a week from the *Nipsey Money* programme. These payments could not last as on Wednesday of that week:

'All the Men in the Shafton Seam received a fortnights notice to leave.'

Their two weeks notice expired on the 19th of April 1905. This latest action put an additional strain on the already stretched resources of the Hemsworth strike committee, as one reporter identified:

'The local committee and others are doing their best for the helpless and innocent victims of the lock-out, the innocent women and children, in providing them with at least sufficient food to stave off the dreaded starvation.'

The strike received little mention for the next few weeks until the Wakefield Express claimed to have been informed by Hemsworth miners union officials that:

'Some occupants of the Colliery Company's Houses in Kinsley have been ejected.'

Given that there is no evidence to support this claim I believe no evictions took place at this time.

Another display of solidarity among miners was given during the union branch meeting held on Thursday the 5th of May when:

'The Barnsley Bed men passed a resolution to turn the Nipsey Money into a fund to provide flour and bread for the wives and children of the Shafton men.'

According to the Hemsworth Express the rationale behind this decision was:

'The Shafton men are in a very desperate condition having had no money for the last fortnight and we hear that it will be another fortnight before there is any likelihood of their getting any. The local miners' committee (sic) are however doing their utmost to obtain food for their unfortunate fellow workmen's families either by begging or by buying on credit." Miners at the Haigh Moor shaft pressed the Y. M. A. officers at Barnsley "to let them give notice to

remedy their existing grievances for non-payment of the price-list by the Colliery Company.'

The support given by the miners of the Barnsley Bed to their colleagues was replicated by other sections of the population: Thomas Ward, Secretary of Kinsley Coronation Working Men's Club:

'Sent an appeal for help to every affiliated Working Men's club in the United Kingdom.'

Mr Ward's appeal must have been successful because the following week the Wakefield Express informed its readers:

'Kinsley Coronation Working Men's Club distributed half a ton of fish to the needy members and the clubs in the surrounding villages have distributed a quantity of flour to those of their members who are out of employment through the Hemsworth lock-out.'

On Monday evening of the 13th of April some 500 men attended an open-air meeting on Cross Hills in Hemsworth, which had been organised by the local Labour Committee. William Bull, Chairman, introduced the invited speakers:

Mr J. Penney: (organiser of the district's Independent Labour Party) told the assembled crowd:

"There was no hope for justice for the workman on disputes with their employers until the working men were proportionally represented on all political bodies and did their part not only in making the laws of the country but in administering them."

Dr Stanton Colt: (prospective parliamentary Candidate for Wakefield) was next on the platform. He delivered a rousing speech lasting almost one hour. In his call for action the main points made were:

He began by: *"Asking men who had been out of work for 9 months due to lock out what they had done with their leisure time.*

Had they organised a meeting or agitated on behalf of themselves or their families and fellow sufferers.

Was it inconceivable that 500 men who are now facing starvation could fully settle the dispute within a month. Let all the men who are locked out of work meet the next morning. Let them organise 1100 men who are now facing starvation and get them to meet on Sunday Morning and march in procession to the Parish Church and to all the Chapels of the surrounding district.

Let them make their claim known to the religious communities; compel the clergy and Ministers of Religion to take up their cause.

Let them organise again and march 11 strong to the meeting place of the Rural District Council and constrain by the justice of their cause the council itself to become the champion of the unemployed. Let the Hemsworth Rural District Council take a stand for the oppressed as the town Council of East Ham had taken a stand in defence of the ratepayers by refusing to administer the Education Act because the rates were unjustly high.

Let them organise relief and get the greatest Labour agitators of the country to Hemsworth, thus the press of the whole nation would echo their cry for justice and the owners of the mine would be compelled by public opinion to do quickly the righteousness which they meant to escape doing at all. The locked men had been living on 9/- per week with 1/- for each child under 14 years of age The men and their families had been half starved and half clothed.

If they loved their children let them begin at once to agitate in this manner, but if they preferred to live on 9/- a week let them go on in the fruitless idleness of the last 9 months."

With the benefit of hindsight it can be seen that this speech was the catalyst which helped change the Hemsworth miners from being mere members of a striking community into becoming a highly organised and disciplined force prepared to use every legitimate means at their disposal in their struggle against the Colliery Company.

The first indication of the strike committee's change in approach came in the week beginning the 15th of May:

'One of the leaders visited all the schools in the district and found many children were being sent to school without breaking their fast while some had no food to go to when they left school. Immediate relief was given as far as practicable.'

Some good news was received on Thursday of the same week when the Y.M.A. at Barnsley informed the Shafton miners they would receive lock-out pay, these:

'Men have had no money coming in for the past month so that they and their wives and families have been on the verge of starvation.'

Following John Potts report on the condition of the miner's children attending the local schools, two deputations were elected, one to lobby the Education Committee, the other comprising School Managers to meet the Board of Guardians to try to get assistance for the underfed schoolchildren.

Chapter Three

The Miners and the Board of Guardians

It is very hard for us to imagine the conditions and feelings of those unfortunates who were confined to the workhouse as a way of receiving help from the Board of Guardians.

The feelings of some of the inmates were scratched on the door of the Hemsworth Workhouse Tramp's Cell:

God bless our King and bless him
although he is old he is in good health
Dukes Earls and Princes by the score
Jewels and riches in galore
he has ships upon the seas and castles on the land
And every thing – its' splendid and grand
The ships upon the seas and castles on the land
Was all made by the working mans hand
Here's to our working man and god bless him
God... the man who pays bad wages.

On the next cell door:

Heaven is higher than a tree
Hell is deeper than the sea
Thunder louder than a horn
Hunger sharper than a thorn

God made the bees
Bees make the honey
Tramps break the stones
Guardians get the money

Walls do not a prison make
Nor Iron bars a cell.

There is another poem from a young woman who committed suicide there:

Here lies a poor woman who was always tired
She lived in a house where help was not hired
Her last words on earth were: Dear friends, I am going
Where washing ain't done, nor sweeping, nor sewing;
But everything there is exact to my wishes;
For where they don't eat there's no washing of dishes.
I'll be where loud anthems will always be ringing,
But having no voice. I'll be clear of the singing.
Don't mourn for me now; don't mourn for me never—
I'm going to do nothing for ever and ever.

Prior to the introduction of the Welfare state the poor and unemployed were dealt with under the Poor Law Amendment Act. This Act created a central authority, the Local Government Board whose officers were charged with overseeing the 650 unions who gave assistance to the destitute in their catchment areas. The Local Unions were overseen by some 500 Guardians. The Board of Guardians generally comprised semi-literate farmers and shopkeepers who were answerable to the ratepayers for their expenditure.

The previous provision of *Outdoor Relief* for the destitute was abolished, Guardians were now required to build a workhouse and ensure the destitute could only have assistance if they entered this facility. The test for applicants for relief was fairly specific their standard of living had to be:

'Worse than the poorest paid independent labourer.'

This strict approach ensured only the genuinely destitute would accept conditions which, in addition to being classed as a pauper meant the loss of freedom and personal status. The underlying philosophy of the policy based on 'The Report of the Commission on the Poor Law of 1832' makes it clear that cases accepted for relief:

'Shall not be made really or apparently so eligible as the situation of the independent labourer of the lowest class.'

The cornerstone of this approach was *The Principle of Less Eligibility* which was based on the belief that state assistance to the poor could not be so generous that people were attracted to it from paid work.

The deputation of School managers from among the ranks of the Hemsworth colliers arranged an interview with the Board of Guardians in the week of the 20th of May 1905. Their primary object was to get assistance for the children under the *Feeding of School Children Order.*

The collier's first visit to the Board of Guardians was unsuccessful:

'The deputation had been mostly without anything to eat from 8 o'clock in the morning until 3.30pm when they left to get some food.'

The Board adjourned for two weeks. During this time Mr Burkitt, the Relieving Officer, compiled reports on 11 of the cases of alleged underfeeding. Mr Burkitt's report refuted the miner's claim:

'All of the cases seem to have been taken without the parents consent and on going round them he found them very indignant. One woman said, it's a lie they ever go without breakfast. Another said they don't want anything.' He concluded by asserting: *'Of the 11 cases reported he found only 4 real cases and they are casual. The deputation should have checked their facts.'*

Mr Burkitt's report provoked an angry response from John Potts, leader of the miner's deputation, who wrote:

'Sir,
Your report of the Hemsworth Guardian meeting held Thursday last with respect to underfed children arising upon the report of Mr Burkitt in connexion with the 11 specific cases handed in by the deputation.

The information was elicited from the children, not alone by me but in the presence of and by the schoolteachers themselves and the document of the 11 specific cases was in the handwriting of the teachers with one solitary exception. I repeat my statement made at the Guardian's meeting and court joint inquiry and challenge investigations. May I ask the Guardians at their next meeting to appoint 4 sensible men inclusive of Mr W.Tempest. J.P along with the recent deputation and we will undertake to not only investigate the above cases, but we will take them to underfed famishing children.

Sir,
Mr Burkitt, personally told me, prior to his enquiries, that he was against us, and that there might be one or two cases but that our statements were without foundation and I am prepared to meet the Board and state time and place where told and, if so allowed I will state certain other information arising upon this matter which will

evidently ease and settle their minds that an impartial inquiry has not been made, neither is Mr Burkitt in my opinion, fit to make inquiry. I have no time to waste over this matter but may I ask that the circular Order no 48675 dated 27th April 1905 and the Relief (School Children) Order is for, as ... to the Guardians by the Local Government Board?

The very essence of the subject matter contained therein is to meet underfed children, and hundreds are practically starving at this moment in the Township of Hemsworth. Whilst the Guardians decide, the report shall lie on the table, which means that further action shall be taken.

As a school Manager I know destitution is most numerous and scores of cases have been relieved, to which must be added the fact that the Miners Committee disbursed £85.0s.0d of flour alone in one week, which prevented numerous applications to the Guardians.

Have the guardians any reason or common sense? If so, let them tell me how we are to exist, let alone live upon 9/- and 1/- each child per week.

I will take the case upon which Mr Burkitt reported the man was indignant, who had restarted work when he went to his neighbours house. The man was indignant who had just restarted. The man drew 21 shillings paid 11 shillings for lodgings brought 10 shillings home, paid 6 shillings for rent and had 4 shillings left to maintain a family of five.

This is the man Mr Burkitt reports was indignant with him. The man has explained to me and three other gentlemen, his position which is at moment, a desperate one: The people are starving in their houses. I am not a believer in Sunday meeting but a meeting will be held on Cross Hills, Hemsworth Sunday night when the Guardians might accept an invitation to discussion and I will stake my reputation that eight out of the 30 odd Guardians know anything about the order.

Probably Mr Green, who seems to have taken the lead in opposition to starving children will put in an appearance and assign his reasons why he took the action he did unless his opposition arose from his usual editable temperament to save the money irrespective of starvation.

John Potts,
Holly Bank,
Hemsworth,
January 21st 1905.

The following Sunday some 700 people attended an open air meeting at Cross Hills to discuss the question of underfed children. Among the points raised was the case of one man who had kept his children from school:

'*So that they could earn money to help the family.*'

The man had been summoned to appear before the court at Pontefract on the 22nd of May:

'*The man was stopped from work by Mr Povey Harper for not taking a reduction in his wage, his girl was kept from school because she was able to earn 2d or 3d at various times. The man was fined 7/6, but has not paid it and cannot do so.*'

After much discussion the assembled group agreed:

'*This meeting regrets the decision arrived at by the Guardians of Hemsworth Poor Law Union to shelve the question of relieving underfed school children in the Township of Hemsworth, contrary to the Local Government Board Order dated 27th April 1905 and places on record, protestation against the Boards method of conducting inquiry into impoverished homes.*

We further call upon the Hemsworth representatives of the said Board to re-open the question upon confirmation of the last meetings minutes and failing thereto they be empowered and requested to petition the Local Government Board.'

On Saturday the 1st of July The Wakefield Express reported on a meeting of the Hemsworth Board of Guardians which had been held on the previous Thursday. During this meeting a letter signed by John Potts and others was read out by the clerk:

'Gentlemen, we desire to be heard in connexion with the insufficient feeding of school children under the Local Government Board Order. The mothers of many children, also the fathers are here awaiting your decision thereon to have their children fed or not. We shall esteem it a favour to be heard as early as possible.'

An interesting discussion showing the differing opinions among the Guardians preceded their decision:

Chairman: "*We don't want to shirk our duty and we don't want those children to pine.*"

Mr Green: "*We don't want the ratepayers imposing upon.*"

Mr Watmough: "*People outside should send in three parents representing the worst cases.*" He relented this later *"as it was not fair to others.*"

Mr Green: "*The representatives who signed this letter should send in a list of the most necessitous cases.*"

Chairman: "*We have not forgotten what happened last time when enquiries were made things were very different to what had been represented. Hemsworth had 4 representatives on the Board. I think it should be through them that the representation should be made.*"

Eventually the Guardians decided to hear each individual case, noting the name and address, number in family, number of children attending school, whether they ever went to school without food, the amount of Miners Union pay coming into the house and the earnings of any members of the family. Fifty-three parents, mainly mothers from the village of Kinsley, were interviewed. In response to the Guardian's question:

'Have your children ever gone to school insufficiently fed?'

The invariable reply was that they the parents had gone short themselves:

'So that the children might have something to eat, if only a little. There was generally only dry bread and fat.' They explained *'they received the miners pay on Thursday and by the following Tuesday or Wednesday there was hardly anything left in the house. It had been no uncommon thing for them to go without breakfast on Thursday morning.'*

The average family had five children which meant 14 shillings per week was their total income. From this, 6 shillings, or in some cases 5 shillings and sixpence, went for rent. In one case the expense of:

'Taking one of the children to Leeds Infirmary once a fortnight had drained the resources and caused the pinch of want to be felt.'

Total income for this household was 11 shillings per week.

After concluding the interviews the Guardians resumed their deliberations.

Mr Watmough: "The *matter should not be shelved and they should deal fairly and squarely with these poor children.*"

Chairman: "*There are some a great deal better off than those on our union books.*"

Mr Haigh: "*Is there not a charity to help these people so that the ratepayers shall not be obliged to do it.*"

Clerk: "*There is no charitable institution because people know that the men can get work at a fair rate of pay if they want.*"

Mr Haigh: "*Would it be advisable to give these children a meal – say on Wednesdays as against their parents receiving their money on the Thursday.*"

Clerk: "*It rests with the Board whether they give children food or not.*"

Chairman: "*The matter is adjourned to the next meeting.*"

The procrastination of the Guardians frustrated the miners who decided to appeal for help at a higher level in the welfare system's hierarchy. To this end:

'*A letter was sent to the Prime Minister, (Mr Arthur Balfour), to Mr Joseph Chamberlain and to a large number of M. P.'s laying the case of the miners of Hemsworth before them intimating that they had applied to the Local Board of Guardians for the putting into force of the Local Government Boards Order No 48175 as to the feeding of children on loan*'.

Whilst the strike committee lobbied for assistance for their children, the Colliery Company increased its pressure on them:

'*On Saturday 22nd of July at Pontefract West Riding Court House Mr G. Lowden applied on behalf of the New Hemsworth Colliery Company for 43 Ejectment Orders in respect of miners tenanting houses situated at Kinsley, the property of the company.*'

In court Mr W. Micholson, (Colliery Traffic Manager), said:

'*He had received instructions from the secretary to serve notices to quit on the respondents.'*

The miner's solicitor argued:

'The company wanted men out not because they did not pay the rent but because they would not work at the colliery.'

Mr Lowden explained: "*the company wanted them ejected because they would not work. If they wanted to work, the summonses would be withdrawn.*"

A touch of humour was brought to the proceedings when the court was informed:

'One witness thought the summons was a picture postcard and even hung it in a frame.'

After deliberation the bench granted Hemsworth Colliery a 21 day *Ejectment Order* in each and every case.

Over the following weeks the Colliery Company applied as much pressure as it could to force the colliers to settle on its terms. At the company's request officers of the Yorkshire Miners Association, accompanied by a deputation of Hemsworth miners, met the Managing Director of the Colliery. After this meeting delegates gave their report at a branch meeting in the Kings Head where members were given the news that the delegation:

'Were told the pits were now closed and nothing could be done.'

In early August whilst the company was telling the miners the pits were now closed, the Wakefield Express drew attention to the duplicitous conduct of the Colliery Company when it reported:

'We are informed that prior to the deputation meeting the Guardians at their meeting a week ago learnt the colliery company had sent a letter to the Clerk stating that all three seams were open for work.'

The action of the Colliery Company added credibility to the statement from one of the strike leaders who claimed:

'This shows clearly that the object in sending the letter was simply to prevent the children being partly fed, by so doing maximum pressure could be applied and the miners forced back to work.'

At a follow up to their meeting with the Board of Guardians a letter explaining the case was sent to the President of the Local Government Board, Mr Gerald Balfour.

Sir
The miners of Fitzwilliam Hemsworth Collieries near Wakefield, instruct us, to place before you the undermentioned facts in connection with the very serious distress prevailing among the Township children, and upon which the Clerk of the Hemsworth Board of Guardians was directed to write to you by their meeting of Thursday last.

On the 27th day of July 1904 the Colliery Company gave 400 Barnsley seam workmen 14 days notice to terminate their contracts of service without assigning any reason whatever, and on the fifth day of April last the Company further gave 700 Shafton workmen additional notices, stating as their reason for doing so that the seam was closed and abandoned, which necessitated the miners appointing a deputation to the Board of Guardians requesting them to adopt the Local Government Boards Circular Order No 14175 dated 27th April 1905 and feed, by loan, the townships underfed school children.

The Education Authority appointed Mr John Potts and Mr Isaac Burns, School Managers, along with the miners deputation to wait upon the Board of Guardians, and on Thursday last for a third time they met, with the ultimate result that the Board decided to place the matter before the Local Government Board, alleging that they might be surcharged for any money spent, which to our mind is nothing less than an attempt to evade putting into operation, your order. They further alleged that the Circular could only be adopted on the requisition of the Educational Authority. To us the Circular is perfectly clear that the guardians have power to feed all underfed children as intended by the Local Government Board's Circular.

The children are not only partially underfed, but are pining as you must observe from the following facts. Take a man with a family – wife and five children. He receives 9/- personally and 1/- for each child, a total of 14/-, less 6d for contributions, leaving 13/6, out of which, prior to purchasing food requisites, deduct rent 7/-, clothing seven persons 2/6, total 9/6, leaving a balance of 4/- per week to maintain the entire family of seven persons. The law is being applied unmercifully to enforce payment of rents.

We petition your Honourable Board to request the Hemsworth Board of Guardians to feed the children, on loan, without delay. Otherwise, there is no alternative but for 300 male persons to make application for ordinary relief, thus disfranchising and pauperising, which we feel confident the Local Government Board wished to avoid when circularising Guardians and School Authorities.'

According to one local newspaper the sentiments expressed in the letter to the President of the Local Government Board reflected the opinions of the people in Hemsworth and Kinsley:

'In this neighbourhood, great indignation is felt at the action of the Board of Guardians in again putting off the feeding question. These people do not want to have to apply for relief in the ordinary way, but if nothing is done they will have to do so and then they will suffer from the stigma of pauperism.'

At the Board of Guardians meeting of the 9th of August discussion continued on the question of underfed schoolchildren:

Clerk: "*I will now read a letter of reply we have received from the Local Government Board in answer to our request for guidance two weeks ago concerning the Board of Guardians liability to feed the children of the miners who are locked out and on strike.*"

The Clerk then read the letter to the Guardians:

'*I am directed by the Local Government Board to acknowledge receipt of your letter on 28th with reference to the question of the relief of children of men on strike.*

I am directed to point out that the operation of the Relief (School Children) Order 1905 is limited to cases in which special application as defined by Article 1 is made to the Guardians.

In that article the term "Special Application" is limited to an application by the Managers' or by a Teacher duly empowered by the Local Education Authority, and having for its object the allowance of relief to a child under the age of 16 who is in course of attendance at a public elementary school.

If therefore the public element schools at which the children attend are (as appears possible) closed for holidays, the order clearly would not apply, and the schools are not so closed, the board would infer from your letter that "no special application" has been made in these cases

If this is so, the Guardians should deal with the case under their general powers.'

The letter evoked an angry response from Messrs Lincoln and Watmough, both of whom were colliers serving on the Board of Guardians:

Cllr Lincoln: "*The Board had ignored the main question. The Clerk's letter had been based on what the Colliery Company said in* *their letter, which was read a fortnight ago. Where did the dispute come in?*

They never asked for a reduction, they said they were going to close the collieries because they could not make them pay. I contend there is no strike. The word strike has nothing to do with it. The Order says Loss of Employment, these people have asked for help because they have lost their employment, not because they are on strike.

Furthermore, the letter says there was no special application, but, was there not a proper application when the School Managers came before the Board?"

Clerk: "*There must be a special application each time. The Local Government Board has evaded the question; we have to make the best of it we possibly can.*"

Chairman: "*The question will have to be settled upon the opinion of the Guardians themselves. When they have done that they will have to abide by the consequences whatever they may be. We have no right to relief of School Children when the parents had voluntarily given up their employment. The affair was so complicated that this was why we wrote to the Local Government Board in the first place.*"

Cllr Lincoln: (heatedly) "*I contend there is no work for these men. The pits were stopped pure and simple, because they could not make them pay. The company never asked the men to go back.*"

Chair: "*The Guardians have the case in their hands.*"

Cllr Lincoln: "*It would never have been discussed if there was not the word Strike put in the clerk's letter.*"

Clerk: "*I did not use the word strike except in strike pay.*"

Cllr Lincoln: "*You say there is plenty of work for the people to go* *to, they have construed it to mean that there is plenty of work and the men are on strike and won't go. This would never have been discussed if there was a strike."*

Cllr Watmough: *"I said last time that there was not a strike. We were given to understand by Mr Fosdick that the Shafton and Barnsley seams were absolutely closed down. It was loss of employment in these seams and the children should be fed."*

Clerk: *"We cannot do anything until the schools are opened."*

Chair: *"This Board are (sic) bound to see their way clear before they do anything."*

Cllr Lincoln: *"Someone has written to the Company but why did they not go to Barnsley also and get their side of the question. It was a deliberate lie that there was any work. There was not.*

The Barnsley Seam had been out just 12 months and most of the men had left the place. Haigh Moor was on strike. Shafton and Barnsley would never work again. I have two letters: one from the Manager, one from the M.D., which had been written to the Miner's Officials testifying to this, and then there was this letter which had been sent to the Board of Guardians, it is a deliberate lie according to those sent to the Union. I take it, they will now have to wait until there is another application from the Education Authority."

Chair: *"This is so, can we now move to other business?"*

The miner's committee as well as being heavily involved in organising relief for the families, fund raising and publicising and seeking support for their case, continued to lobby and apply pressure on the Board of Guardians. Subsequently it was reported on the 26th of August that on completion of their normal business the clerk had informed the Guardians:

'We have Mr Chairman a letter from the School Manager which the Board must hear, because the letter of reply has been sent.' He then proceeded to read: *'We intend making a Special Application to the Board of Guardians on Thursday next to feed, on loan, the whole of the school children belonging to the unemployed workmen, such application of feeding to date from September 4th next upon re-opening of the township schools. We should be glad to hear from you whether your Board will grant the deputation such interview, otherwise we shall be obliged to acquiesce in 1000 people seeking ordinary relief at an early date, as the parents can little longer proceed without.'*

The Guardians replied agreeing to meet the deputation as requested. On the agreed date Isaac Burns and John Potts, both School Managers, accompanied by Wm. Bull, J. Garbutt, J. J. Green, E. Feriday and A. Goddard, attended the Board of Guardians meeting:

Mr Potts: "*Mr Burns and myself as school managers contend that a special application had been made for feeding the children. We have not tabulated the whole of the children, but we ask the Board now to make some arrangements to feed the whole of the children on the re-opening of the schools, until such time as the people are in the position to feed their own children.*

The suffering is very severe therefore we are asking for the immediate relief on the re-opening of schools. If the relief was not given the Board would have 1,000 children or thereabouts to relieve. A number of children are being practically housed and fed by Mr Elstone of Kinsley and in such cases as these they were asking for no relief whatsoever. We only want the Guardians to assist in those cases voluntary help cannot reach. Only where they have no chance of helping the cases do we ask the aid of the Board. We also ask you (without tabulating names) to lay down a system of feeding the whole of the children of the Township. We would prefer it if the Guardians themselves undertook to feed the children but, if the Board do not care to do so, we, as school managers will accept the responsibility, provided the Board supplied the necessary means and settled all accounts. If the Board however decided to do nothing then a special application would be made and every case tabulated. If the Board do not proceed with the whole of the cases, we ask that these tabulated" (passes the list to the chairman) *"be attended to as soon as possible. Mr Burns and myself make this present application in our private capacity as School Managers. The Order said School Managers and application could be made to the Guardians or to the Relieving Officer. We as managers could delegate the matter to the schoolteachers, and authorise them under the Order to seek relief. But we prefer to do it direct and the Guardians to put the Order into force."*

Chair: *"Do the parents of any of these children work?"*

Potts: *"The parents involved all work when there is work for them to go to in all 3 seams at the colliery."*

Chair: *"Which schools do yourself and Mr Burns represent?"*

Potts: *"We represent the whole of the schools as we are members of the Education Sub-Committee."*

Members of the press as well as the deputation of colliers were asked to leave the room whilst the Guardians debated the issue. On their return the miner's deputation was informed:

Chair: *"The schools do not open again until the first Monday of September. I do not see how we can consider the matter until our next meeting which will be September 9th."*

Mr Burns: *"The children will be at school before the Board meets again and the children are severely in need."*

Chair: "*There are no School Children at present, you must bring the matter up when they are at school and underfed.*"

Burns: "*We expected it to be put in hand before the children broke up at all. In the interests of the children, we think you ought to do something.*"

Chair: "*There is no desire to shelve the matter, several of the Guardians have expressed themselves willing to go on with the matter.*"

Potts: "*When we come in a fortnight can we take it for granted that the thing will then be put in operation without any further delay?*"

Chair: "*We shall want to make special investigation ourselves. We would not pay the money without proper investigation into every case.*"

Mr Lincoln: (questioningly) "*We have discussed it, and come to the conclusion that whatever crops up the Guardians are willing to feed the children when proper application is made?*"

Chair: "*We make no promises whatever; when it comes before us in a fortnight we will discuss it.*"

Mr Lincoln: "*I take it that as Guardians, in a fortnights time we are not going to shirk our responsibility, and if the children are underfed we are prepared to do our duty and feed them?*"

Mr Tyas: "*It has been suggested that at the next meeting of the Board the managers should bring up a list showing the children in the township, the amount of money the parents are receiving from all sources and the total number of children in each family. Maybe they should also differentiate between a large and a small family.*"

Mr Lincoln: "*One suggestion was that a sub-committee be formed to investigate the affair before the school was re-commenced.*"

Mr Burns: "*There are scores of children who would not attend school until they could be provided with something to eat. The parents have sworn not to send them. We are willing to give the Board any help they need but we hoped that the matter would have been settled that day. It would considerably lessen the attendance at school re-opening, if something were not done at once. We had also hoped that a small committee would be appointed that day and that we had been at considerable trouble to get that list to the Board.*"

Clerk: "*They do not come under the Order at all because they are not at school.*"

Mr Potts: "*I am not satisfied. I hold we are still within our rights arising upon the resolution that has been recorded by the Education Sub-Committee. There has been nothing done and we were thus within our rights and these rights have not ceased to exist.*

We know the Board has no power to feed the children at present, but they have the power to take proceedings. They could commence making arrangements in readiness for when the children go back to school. The Order does not debar you from doing that."

The chairman then adjourned the meeting for 2 weeks. During this time Potts and Burns prepared their case and canvassed for support, as the local paper revealed:

'*John Potts and Ike Burns have secured additional school managers to join them in their appeal for the feeding of the children when the matter comes up next Thursday at the meeting of the Board of Guardians. During the past week, the two men have been busy collecting facts for the meeting. They will be armed with names and addresses of the parents of 900 school children, the actual amount of money coming in to the family from all sources and the total number in family.*

They are determined to win their case next week; no stone will be unturned until they achieve this end.'

Following their last meeting with the Board of Guardians the miners expected the issue of providing assistance in feeding the children would be re-considered when the schools re-opened. In expectation of this the miner's deputation waited outside the meeting room. However, on finishing the normal business of the Board, the Chairman, Mr C. J. Tyas, declared the meeting closed. This procedure was questioned by the colliers serving as members of the Board.

Cllr Watmough: "*Has no intimation been received that a deputation was expecting to interview the Board? Mr Potts and his friends are waiting outside.*"

Mr Burkitt: "*Has no notification been received from the school managers on the underfed children question?*"

Clerk: "*I have received no notice either verbal or (sic) in writing.*"

Chair: "*That is all the business gentlemen.*"

On hearing this John Potts and his colleagues were angered at not being given a hearing. They had previously submitted the most urgent cases requiring assistance before the Board and were at a loss as to how the children of these families were to be fed. Turning their attention to the press:

Mr Burns: "*It will be impossible for the people to last out until the next meeting; they will have to invade the Relieving Officers House with a thousand people.*"

John Potts: "*Here is the detail of the cases we have given the Board: In 56 families there were 268 children, 184 of whom attended school. Total income for these families for 1 week was £37.19.9d out of which came rent of £14.15.9d, Clothing, Light, Coal and*

Incidentals £7.10.6d. This left only about 2/6d per house to keep a family of five in food. Only £15.3.6d was thus left for feeding 377 people for a week, working out at 9½d (nine pence hapenny) for each person for one week's food. Thus the question was: Is it possible for a person to live on less than 10d per week?"

At the Board of Guardians meeting on Thursday the 22nd of September John Potts and Ike Burns, accompanied by H. Goddard and J. J. Green, appeared to reiterate their appeal for a loan to help feed the school children.

Potts: "*I do not intend making a long statement but will merely repeat that they were in exactly the same position as on the prior occasions, except that, looking from the clerk's view of the matter they were formally not in order. We hold that we are in the right but the clerk seemed to expect an application from them prior to our going before the Board.*

I would like to impress upon the Board that they as School Managers could come to the Board at any time and ask for relief when they found distress cases. We came on the last occasion and after waiting an hour were denied a hearing, I have no hesitation in saying the Board knew we were outside... Must stress again we are not compelled to give notice of our intention to come before the Board; but as a matter of courtesy they desired to do it.

I now ask the Board to feed these children who are underfed. I know it might be said, on the Boards side, that as far as their information went they were not aware that any poverty existed, for your information, we have prepared a sheet which showed... the position of 56 cases."

(The figures quoted by John Potts were those given previously to the press following the last Board of Guardians meeting.)

"We ask the Board to feed them in a systematic way. The question might be raised that it would be a serious cost to the rates, but at the same time, they were Guardians of the poor first and Guardians of the public purse second. The Guardians are compelled to feed these people and we do not want the Guardians to get away from that fact."

Chair: "*You must leave us to our own judgement.*"

Cllr Clough: "*Mr Potts is laying down the Law.*"

John Potts: "T*he Guardians at Merthyr Tydfil were taken to court for refusing to put the Order into force. We expect the Guardians to do something practical.*"

Chair: "*You must allow us our own judgement.*"

Ike Burns: "*We are simply laying the matter before you so that you will be able to use your judgement.*"

John Potts: "*There is one family with 11 children attending school; their income is 19/6d, rent equals 6/- per week, fire and clothing for 13 people 4/-, leaving 9/6d to feed 13 people a week. It simply cannot be done.*"

Chair: "*You are not forgetting this is a circumstance that has been brought about voluntarily. That is the thing we have to consider.*"

Potts: "*I don't know what you mean by voluntarily.*"

Chair: "*I mean that the men threw their work up… I say that is a voluntary action.*"

Potts: "*The argument may be a sensible one to your point of view but it is not law. The Law says:*"

Interruption:

Chair: *"When we want to know the law, we shall ask our clerk."*

Cllr Watmough: *"You ought to allow Mr Potts to make a statement."*

Potts: *"If you mean to be unfair to us, we have a remedy equally with the Guardians. We do not want to resort to the Law. The point I want to impress upon yourself and the Board is you are compelled by Law to feed these children irrespective of strike or stoppage, you say this is a point.*

We ask you to put the Law into motion and feed the children, on ascertained facts. We will give you all the help we possibly can. We don't want to spend money insensibly.

We do want the children feeding and we expect it."

Clerk: *"Have the School Managers at a meeting, authorised you to come here?"*

Potts: *"Our authority lies in our appointment. We have not been appointed at a meeting."*

Burns: *"I do not like the hostile attitude in which we have been received."*

Chair: *"You can't expect people to meet you if you come here and say we are meeting you in a hostile manner."*

Burns: *"Mr Potts has proved to any open-minded individual that there is a need for the Order to be put into force. There clearly is a need for an Order when the Rector (Rev Gilbert) was feeding 250 children per week and Mr T. Elstone 53 daily.*

With regard to finances, we merely ask for a loan. The Board could get the money back; it is not so serious a financial matter. I hope you will take it in hand.

If you come with me through the schools, I will show you underfed children and will also show you some who were at home because of an insufficiency of food."

The collier's deputation and reporters left the room whilst the Guardians considered the case. After some 30 minutes they were allowed back:

Chair: "*I have to say that after serious and rather lengthy consideration, the Board have by a unanimous vote decided that your application for feeding the children generally in the township of Hemsworth, be refused.*"

Potts: "*Are we to take it sir that the application is decidedly refused?*"

Chair: "*You may say that it is.*"

Potts: "*On what grounds?*"

Chorus of Guardians: "*No. No.*"

Potts: "*I feel very sorry indeed that you the Board have come to that decision. I would like to know what is to become of the people of the township. Only this afternoon they the Board had given the Order for the house of a woman who had been left destitute by the death of her husband who had worked 25 years in the district. These destitute people are coming to us and we are unable to help them. They shall be obliged to go elsewhere.*

I can only say we shall have to reconsider your decision and I don't like to disappoint anybody, I believe we shall lodge a summons against yourself Mr Chairman."

Chorus: of *'Hear Hear.' Laughter* from the members.

Chair: "*I shall be here.*" *Laughter.*

Potts: *"May the tabular statement we gave you be returned."*

Clerk: *"We shall keep it as one of our records in case legal proceedings were taken."*

Although unsuccessful in getting assistance from the Board of Guardians, Potts and Burns continued to fight for the rights of underfed schoolchildren, gaining support for their fight throughout the whole of the emerging labour movement. Indeed many of the welfare reforms they had argued for were encompassed in the Liberal welfare reforms of 1906.

The Yorkshire Coal Owners Association

Whilst giving the appearance of playing a very minor part in this particular strike, the Yorkshire Coal Owners Association played a significant part in events prior to and during the dispute. The Coal Owner's role on the Conciliation Board provides a good example of the use of power and influence ensuring the primary interests of the Association were advanced and protected.

It is important to understand the role of the Coal Owners Association during industrial disputes in their industry. It assumes the role of conciliator on the Conciliation Board as well as paymaster to its members; roles similar to those of the Yorkshire Miners Association which acted as both the conciliator and paymaster during strikes and lock-outs involving its members. Although the Association responds to pressure from both sides, it is more attentive to pressure from its own members. In an attempt to show this I have included extracts from minutes of their meetings held during the early stages of the Hemsworth dispute.

Formal notification of the dispute affecting the Fitzwilliam Hemsworth Colliery was given at a special council meeting held on the 25th of July. During this meeting the Secretary informed members of a letter from Fitzwilliam Hemsworth Collieries Ltd. stating that men employed in the Haigh Moor seam had given 14 days notice to terminate their engagement with effect from the 2nd of August. In this letter Mr Fosdick claimed:

'He was not aware that the men had any grievances. He had not been asked to meet any deputation and he could not suggest any reason for the dispute.

He said the members were aware the company had some time ago closed their Barnsley and Shafton seams, the former in consequence of depressed trade and the latter on account of the seam being worked out.'

A further special meeting of the Coal Owners Association was held on the 1st of August to discuss the threatened strike at the Haigh Moor seam. The Chairman, Mr Currer Briggs, outlined a conversation he had with Mr Wadsworth of the Y.M.A. after the previous Joint Board meeting. According to Currer Briggs, Mr Wadsworth confirmed the miners would not withdraw their notices unless Mr Fosdick agreed to re-open the Barnsley Seam on the old terms, as recommended by the Umpire. Since Mr Fosdick would not entertain this suggestion the matter ended there.

The chairman then read an extract from the minutes of 1901 relating to the price list of the Colliery Company, explaining that *The Price* fixed by the umpire Mr Atkinson was the *Fixed Getting Price* within the meaning of the *Deed of Association,* therefore if the Fitzwilliam Hemsworth Colliery Company were paying in accordance with the awarded price list they would be entitled to the support of the Association in the event of a strike.

Percy Greaves read extracts from a letter from Mr Higson, Consulting Engineer at Hemsworth Colliery Ltd, to Mr Wadsworth on the 15th of February 1905. In this letter:

'He had asked for a meeting with miner's officials to discuss the question of a reduction in the prices in the Barnsley and Haigh Moor seams or alternatively closing of the pits.'

Mr Hargreaves, solicitor for the Hemsworth Company, claimed:

'The letter would be written without the authority of the Board.'

After debate it was decided to adjourn proceedings until Mr Percy Greaves and Mr Scott met with officers of the Y.M.A. to discuss the circumstances surrounding the strike.

On the 23rd of August the Report from Greaves and Scott on their meeting with the Y.M.A. on the 15th of August informed the Association of the miner's grievance which was:

'Management had refused to carry out and pay in accordance with 8 clauses in the price list now in force for the Haigh Moor seam.'

Currer Briggs then read out a letter from John Wadsworth of the Y.M.A. dated the 16th of August, informing the Coal Owners Association a meeting had been held with the Hemsworth miners who were ready to restart working if the Company agreed to pay the awarded prices plus the arrears owed. Indeed the miners had commenced legal proceedings against the Colliery Company for the recovery of the arrears of pay.

Once again Mr Fosdick denied any knowledge of the men's grievances. Currer Briggs responding to Richard Fosdick's statement, praised the miner's efforts in trying to remedy the situation and informed Fosdick that as a result of the Association's enquiries they would have to reconsider its position vis a vis the Colliery Company.

At a further meeting of the Coal Owners Association held on the 26th of September the Chairman outlined the sequence of events leading to the Haigh Moor strike; in so doing he clarified the Association's current position:

'Members were bound by their Deed of Association, if it was shown that the Company was in breach of the Deed in refusing to

implement the arbitrator's pay award, the Association's liability to pay their indemnity would cease. The Company must thoroughly understand that in the event of not complying with the requirements of the Association, they would not be entitled to further support.'

Fosdick argued that by terminating their employment and taking strike action the miners had effectively cancelled the Arbitrator's pay award. As a consequence the Company absolutely declined to reopen the pit under the old price list.

Currer Briggs reiterated the Association's dilemma:

'In view of his promises to the Miners Officials at the last meeting of the Joint Committee that if the men withdrew their notices unconditionally he would use his influence with the Company to allow them to resume work.'

After much discussion a compromise resolution was reached which stated:

'If the Hemsworth Colliery Company would relinquish all claims to indemnity from this day week, a meeting of the Joint committee might be convened, at which the Miners Officials should be informed that the Company could not afford to re-open the pit on the Old Price list. But, that the Association was prepared to recommend the owners to negotiate for a new price list.'

In so doing the Coal Owners Association denied Fosdick's company the financial support due to its members undergoing industrial disputes whilst appearing to give its moral support. The Association's Secretary was then instructed to carry out the terms of the arrangement:

'Without the passing of a formal resolution.'

The formal resolution merely stating:

'The miners section of the Joint committee be asked again to meet the Owners section of that Committee with a view to bringing about a settlement of the strike.'

The manoeuvre outlined above enabled the Association to limit its indemnity payment to a member company to a total of £1,413-6s-8d.

'That sum being in full satisfaction of all claims for indemnity against the Association in respect of the existing Strike.'

Given that the strike lasted a total of ten years, it could be argued that the Association made a prudent decision.

I am not suggesting the Yorkshire Coal Owners Association were always and everywhere against cutting miner's wages. Indeed on the 27th of September, roughly two weeks after reaching its decision on the Hemsworth Company, the same association unanimously supported a resolution from its National Association proposing:

'Miners wages should be reduced by 5%' because *'the selling price of coal up to last July was 6d per ton below the price prevailing when the last reduction in wages had been obtained.'*

Later that month Currer Briggs, Chairman of the C.O.A., reported on the meeting of the National Conciliation Board held on the 12th, during which it was felt Lord James (the Umpire) was not in favour of the proposed reduction in miner's wages.

The matter had subsequently been reconsidered in the Owners Section of the Conciliation Board meeting of the 19th, where it was decided that a proposed lesser reduction of two and an half pence (2½d) per ton would not be accepted by the miners, nor by Lord James. The members finally agreed wages should remain unchanged until March 1906. Whilst agreeing with the national board's course of action the Yorkshire Coal Owners representatives would not support any time element being included in the proposition. This was done simply to ensure they retained their normal practice of reducing miner's wages in line with reductions in the selling price of their coal.

In summary, the Yorkshire Coal Owners Association's role on the Trade Conciliation Boards was in essence a balancing act. The raison d'etre for their existence was to protect and advance the interests of its members whilst at the same time giving the impression of being fair minded. Indeed it could even be argued that the Organisation's need for survival outweighed the interests of its individual members. From this viewpoint its involvement with the unions in the Joint Conciliation Boards can best be described as a form of *Unenlightened Self Interest.*

Chapter Four

The Evictions

In West Riding Court House, Pontefract, on the 22nd of July 1905 the New Hemsworth Colliery Company solicitor applied for:

'43 ejectment orders in respect of miners tenanting houses situated at Kinsley, the property of the company.'

The company's case was simple; if the men were on strike they had broken their contract therefore they were not entitled to live in housing provided by the company:

'If they would do work the summonses would be withdrawn.'

In every case the magistrates granted a 21 day ejectment order on the Kinsley tenants.

When the summons were issued they caused a mixture of anger and fear for most of the colliers and their families, as ever there were exceptions, in this case one poor man unable to read or write:

'Thought the summons was a picture postcard and even hung it in a frame.'

By the beginning of August the entire colliery was at a standstill with colliers in Haigh Moor ceasing to work and all 50 pit ponies being pulled out and put to graze. Again the stated cause was the company's refusal to honour the Umpire's recommendations. The action of the Haigh Moor colliers brought the number of unemployed miners to 1600 including some 700 members of The National and International General Federation of Trade and Labour Unions.

At the Joint Board meeting of the same week the Chairman, Currer Briggs, asked the Board to look into the dispute at Hemsworth with a view to finding a resolution. Likewise the issue was raised at the Y.M.A. meeting which instructed Messrs Hall, Jacks, Kelley and Walsh to meet with the Hemsworth miners and to see if it was possible to find a solution. The deputation addressed a meeting of the Hemsworth men in the Kings Head Inn to inform them that they had interviewed Mr Fosdick and the manager, Povey Harper, only to be told:

'The pits were now closed and nothing could be done.'

A report in the local newspaper on the 5th of August informed the world the company had applied for a further 90 ejection orders bringing the total number to 170.

To provide accommodation for the families from these houses the miner's committee had been negotiating with local landowners, or their tenants, trying to obtain consent to erect tents to accommodate the evicted families. Some support came from mining colleagues in Scotland who forwarded £25 to help the families in Hemsworth.

Within the Yorkshire mining industry in this period eviction from tied housing was commonly used as a bargaining tool during industrial disputes, thereby exerting maximum pressure on the workers.

In anticipation of the actions of the miners the Colliery Company contacted local landowners advising them not to help the miners by allowing them to erect tents on their land. As a consequence of this request one of the local landowners is reported to have given instructions to his tenants that:

'No land belonging to me is to be let for camping purposes.'

In desperation the miner's committee cast their net further afield; John Potts had written to Boddingtons Brewers of Manchester, owners of the Kinsley Hotel, asking permission to erect a tent on the *Old Football Field* adjoining the hotel. Boddingtons regretted the situation in the neighbourhood, hoped the strike would soon be over their difficulties settled, then refused the miner's request to use the land.

In a further step to put pressure on the colliers the Coal Company had written to the Board of Guardians, according to the local newspaper:

'We are informed that prior to the deputation meeting with the Guardians.... The Colliery Company had sent a letter to the clerk stating that all the three seams were open for work.'

The report continued by including the views of one of the local union leaders to his news:

'This shows clearly that the object in sending the letter was simply to prevent the children being partly fed.'

The company's letter was used by the Board of Guardians to deny the miners assistance on the grounds that work was available for them. A detailed account of the Board's handling of the miner's application and indeed the miner's response to this is included as a separate section, mainly to remind one of the difficulties in obtaining social assistance prior to the introduction of the welfare state.

Whilst waiting on a decision from the Board of Guardians local miners, with the approval of the strike committee, formed the

Hemsworth Locked Out Miners Children Relief Fund Committee whose objective was to raise money to buy clothes and boots for the miner's children in the way the Welsh miners had done during the Bethesda strike.

Despite the efforts of the Colliery Company to prevent land being used to accommodate the evicted families the strike committee were successful in obtaining a field where they could erect the tents which would become *Home* for the evicted families. Unfortunately as the following extract shows, it was less than desirable:

'The Brickyard in Kinsley has been secured and a camp for twenty five tents is to be erected there. The place is far from being an ideal one but unfortunately no other is available. Alongside the ground, which lies between the last row of houses and the railway there is a large duck pond, which also appears to be the repository for all kinds of rubbish. The pond is fed by several small streams, and one or two of them run into a beck beside the railway, opposite to the station. One of the streams resembles black ink or dye rather than water, and certainly appears in a much worse condition than even the polluted rivers of the West Riding. There is also a large plantation of oslers and bulrushes. It will be very hard indeed for the people if they are obliged to stay in such a place all through the winter, where the dampness would render them susceptible to all manner of diseases. But as we have said there seems to be no other available site in the whole district and the best will have to be made of the accommodation they have got.'

As the day of the evictions drew near local miner's leaders, aware of the depth of anger and resentment felt by the colliers and their families, advised those being made homeless to leave quietly and not resist the police who would be used to remove them and their possessions from the colliery houses. The miner's committee contacted both the Mayor of Wakefield and General Booth of the Salvation Army requesting them to come as witnesses to the evictions, and to provide spiritual support to their ranks. Colliers not under threat of eviction rallied to assist their neighbours by storing their furniture and household goods.

While these events were taking place new depths of poverty became increasingly visible. As one reporter informed his readers, the school children in the village were:

'Beginning to show signs of feeling the effect of the stoppage and the majority of them are going about in rags and with hardly any boots or shoes whilst in some cases they are wearing no boots at all.'

To relieve the financial hardship in the village a choir comprising: W. Mills, T. Craddock, M. Morriss, G. Harrison (violin), E. Richards, Wm Guy, A. Kenning accompanied by I Bailey (portable Harmonium) and J. Aupit (Secretary) were despatched to Mexbororough, Houghton, Thurnscoe, Wath and Wombwell. Two more choirs were already rehearsing in the local Gospel mission getting ready to visit villages in the Wakefield and Pontefract areas.

A few of the miners enjoying the break from work, if not the lack of pay and threat of eviction, passed their time less constructively. As a consequence of two of these leisure pursuits Wm. Mills and Ernest Richards were both fined 4 shillings for playing football in the streets. Thomas Orme, Robert Goulding, Robert Waite and Michael Cosgrove were fined between 10 shillings and 16 shillings and 6 pence with 9 shillings costs for playing at *Banker* with cards.

On the 14th of August Mr Betts, a well known lay preacher and land and property owner with houses in New Street, Bond Street and King Street as well as land known as the *Old Brickyard*, issued his miner tenants with: '*7 days notice to quit*'. Of the 91 cottages Betts owned, 84 were subject of notice to quit, the other houses were excluded. Four of these houses provided accommodation for Belgian workers employed at the coking ovens, another housed a tenant who had previously submitted a *Valuation Claim,* whilst the remainder housed tenants who were ill.

To make matters worse Mr Betts who had previously given the miners permission to erect tents on the *Old Brickyard,* had his solicitor write to the miner's committee via Edgar Cuthbert:

'Dear Sir

12th August 1905

We have been consulted by Mr Henry Betts the owner of the Brickyard in New Street, Kinsley, with reference to the permission he gave you a few days ago to occupy this brickyard temporarily for the purpose of camping out evicted tenants from the colliery property in question. Since this promise was given an offer has been made to Mr Betts for the tenancy of the property in question and Mr Betts having accepted such an offer, it is necessary for him to determine the permission given to you. Will you therefore kindly take notice that the premises must not be used or occupied by you in any way.'

Undeterred by Betts' action the strike committee eventually secured a piece of land near the gas works. Under the watchful eyes of a crowd of onlookers a bell tent was erected to allow the committee to experiment with the laying of flooring:

'To reduce condensation and increase comfort for its future occupants.'

On Tuesday morning around 10 o'clock the village woke up as normal. A rumour that the evictions, expected to begin on Wednesday or Thursday, would take place that very day circulated the village. In anticipation of the arrival of the police to carry out the evictions groups of angry miners gathered on the roadways.

Just after ten o'clock in the morning the blue coats and helmets of a posse of police were seen descending the hill leading into the village. As the marching line of blue came into view a cry went up from a crowd of watching youngsters:

'T' Bobbies are coming.'

The miners rushed to the centre of the village as the mob of children and mothers went to meet the police and welcome them with hoots and yells.

Arriving at New Row the twenty five policemen delegated to carry out the evictions were split into two groups: Inspector Sykes and his men were detailed to empty 19 houses in Kinsley Terrace, Gorton Terrace and Longsight Terrace, Inspector Hartley's men detailed to evict the 24 families in New Row and Outgang Terrace.

In one house a burly policeman who had been helping to carry some heavy and dusty furniture *'began daintily'* to blow the dust off his coat and hands when a woman in the crowd cried out:

'Sitha! He's freetened on a wee bit o' muck.'

One old woman with tears in her eyes cried:

'Its all very fine for t' young uns but what is it for us who have lived here nearly all our lives.'

Another shouted:

'It's 28 years since we were turned out at Sharlston.'

After five and a half hours of hard labour the police finished their unpleasant task, reformed into their marching order and returned to the police station in Hemsworth accompanied by a chorus of hooting and booing from the hordes of women and children.

In anticipation of the evictions the strike committee had erected temporary accommodation consisting of twenty five tents arranged with military precision on the vacant land near the gas works. Among the twenty five tents was a large marquee designated for use as a cook-house and dining area during the day and an entertainment centre at night. At this time cooking facilities comprised only two open stoves; it had been arranged to install proper apparatus later that week.

As the first occupants of the tented village moved in on Tuesday the 15th of August, the younger children had great fun *'playing at houses'* in their new family homes, whilst the older ones entertained themselves by using the vacant land on the site as a cricket pitch.

In an effort to reduce areas of possible conflict as well as maintaining order and discipline within the camp, the relief committee had drawn up:

'Rules of Conduct

The following rules drawn up for the guidance of tent dwellers. The committee expresses the hope that they will be diligently observed.

Each person belonging to a tent is instructed to keep clean in and around his tent and not to allow any refuse of any description to be strewn about. The committee insist that it shall be taken up and placed in a tub provided for that purpose and forbids the throwing of slops in front of the tents.

Parents are requested to keep their children from committing any nuisance on the grounds, and from doing any damage to the ropes and tents.

Obscene language is strictly prohibited on the grounds. Drinking in the tents is a violation of the committee's arrangements, and anyone allowing this to be done will be summoned to appear before the committee and dealt with accordingly.

No person is allowed to solicit in any way from visitors on the camp grounds as sheets are provided for that purpose.

Visitors are requested to leave the tents and grounds at 9 o'clock P.M.

By Order
The Relief Committee
T. Watmough. (Secretary)'

In communities such as mining villages perhaps as a consequence of working in close and highly dangerous conditions, a deep sense of camaraderie and mutual support appear to be integral parts of the social relationships among miners and their families. Thus:

'At a meeting of the miners who worked the Barnsley and Shafton seams it was unanimously decided to hand over their Nipsey Money to their brethren of the Haigh Moor seam.'

Tom Elstone, landlord of the Kinsley Hotel, provided accommodation in the pub ballroom for children between the ages of 5 and 10 years, although fairly basic the children did sleep on straw beds and were given breakfast and dinners by Mr Elstone. To assist him miner's wives ensured that two women were on duty every night as *Temporary Mothers.* To fund his charitable work Tom Elstone made a special appeal for funds and donations of cast-off clothing from members of the public. His appeal was echoed by Mrs Potts who volunteered to carry out any necessary repairs and ensure that clothing was properly distributed.

As well as organising appeals for assistance, travelling choirs and aid for their neediest members, the committee continued to work to ameliorate conditions in the camp, as the Wakefield Echo noted:

'To provide cooking facilities in the large marquee cooking ranges have been installed. Gas has now been laid on. The wood floors

built for the tents keep very dry and are much appreciated. The tents stood the high wind last Saturday remarkably well, and no one yet has begun to complain of the conditions of life in the camp.'

An additional 6 children from evictions which took place later that week were added to the group being cared for in the local pub. As well as providing meals for all the children the Elstone family had to bake 4 stones of flour each day to feed their little guests. The children's dining arrangements were well regimented, breakfast of tea, bread and butter was served at 8am, dinner at precisely 12.00 noon when each child received a soup plate filled with potatoes and a savoury stew plus a piece of bread. Clearing up and cleaning after meals being done by Mr Elstone and 6 male volunteers.

Planning for the worst yet hoping for the best the relief committee had obtained leases on land behind the Co-op and Working Men's Club which would enable them to house a further 200 families if necessary. To ensure every available space was used to provide accommodation the Mission Hall in Kinsley initially used to store furniture, now housed 7 families.

At the end of August some 1900 miners attended a meeting where they were updated on negotiations on the dispute between the Coal Owners and officers of the Yorkshire Miners Association. The Y.M.A. officers asked for, and duly received, the miners support for the following resolution:

'The Hemsworth Haigh Moor men be recommended to offer to withdraw their notices and resume work on the printed price list without prejudice to any matters in court between the Company and the men or any monies owing.'

Prior to the meeting being closed miners from the Barnsley and Shafton seams expressed their willingness to go back to work under the same terms and conditions.

After the meeting John Wadsworth on behalf of the Y.M.A. asked members of the press:

'*Will you please make it known also that the Miners Association are very pleased with the manner and conduct of the Hemsworth Miners and that if the men are to continue fighting on the price list, the officials hope and trust that not only the miners generally, but the public at large will render them all the assistance they can?*'

The relief committee continued to seek assistance from every available avenue; visitors to the village curious to see the children's accommodation were requested to make a donation to help buy food. At the entrance to the tented villages collecting sheets for cash were slung beneath a huge sign imploring passers-by to '*Remember the Evicted.*'

By the end of August three choirs were touring the Barnsley district whilst others toured the Huddersfield area, raising both awareness of the dispute and generating support and much needed donations to help the miner's families. A further six choirs were rehearsing in readiness to broadcast their cause in Goole, York, Halifax and Doncaster.

To ensure transparency and accountability each choir had credentials signed by J. J. Green (committee secretary), the public were asked not to give donations to anyone who could not show these credentials. In their appeal for cast-off clothing and boots the committee asked that anyone wishing to make a donation who lived within a ten mile radius of Hemsworth contact: '*J. J. Green at 29 Bond Street, Kinsley*', by letter or postcard to arrange collection. Other donations should be sent to the Secretary of the relief Fund: '*Gabriel Price, 28 Bond Street, Hemsworth*', cheques made payable to the Treasurer: '*William Wainwright, 40 West Street, Hemsworth.*'

To reinforce both accountability and transparency the committee published weekly balance sheets giving the following information, i.e.:

'Monies Received.	*£70-0s-0d*
Nipsey Money.	*£25-0s-0d*
Travel Expenses to delegates Scotland and England.	*£11-11s-0d*
Railway Fares and Collecting Expenses.	*£26-5s-0d'*

The Independent Labour Party brought its support and radical working class political philosophy into the dispute at Kinsley. One of its members, Miss Isabella Ford, visited the camp giving support, encouragement and cheer to the families. A small but growing band of I.L.P. supporters and sympathisers hastily arranged a *Platform Meeting* where Miss Ford gave a talk on *Socialism and Politics* with the main focus of her address being:

'The greed of the employers and the apathy of the working classes to their own interests.'

Her speech ended by telling the strikers:

'If there was anything to be remedied, it would have to be done by the workers themselves.'

The police were in action the following week as nine more families were scheduled for eviction. It was an easy day for the policemen as five families had already vacated their houses. Of the remaining four one contained a young sick child, on production of a doctor's certificate the family were left in situ. The remaining three were emptied in a mere three quarters of an hour.

In the tented village it was decided to spare the elderly the rigours of camp life by housing them with friends and families in housing not rented from the coal company or its allies. The timing of this

EVICTED CHILDREN
AT DINNER
KINSLEY HOTEL
SEPT 15TH 1905

decision seemed perfect as heavy rainstorms pelted the village on both Friday and Saturday:

'*Rain came through the tents, and soon everything including bedding had received a thorough soaking, and few of the people escaped a wetting.*'

Since the camping ground was below the level of the main sewers it was submerged by water, turning it into an unpleasant quagmire.

The miner's struggle began to be reported in the *London Newspapers* particularly *The Daily News* which gave detailed and accurate accounts of the situation. This growing publicity helped by the dry and bright weather brought thousands of spectators to the area, as these visitors entered the village they were greeted by hordes of children:

'*Going through the time honoured performance of turning cartwheels with the usual request of Chuck us a penny Mister.*'

Once again Kinsley had the vibrancy of a bustling, prosperous village:

'*Cycles and wagonettes were to be seen everywhere, with here and there a camera fiend on the lookout for an interesting snapshot, but it was impossible to get an effective photo.*'

Reporting on the camp itself, one reporter noted how:

'*One was struck by the quiet and orderly appearance of the place and people.*'

The discipline and organisation of the camp was reinforced as *The Curfew Rattle* informed visitors it was time to leave.

Work continued to make the tented village as comfortable as possible, trenches were dug to allow surface water to drain away, six new water closets had been erected and a tap installed obviating the need for residents to fetch water from nearby houses.

The continued appeals by the Relief Committee brought parcels from Manchester, Royston and Wakefield; miners from Allerton Bywater Colliery approved a grant of £8 per week for the next four weeks with a promise that the matter would be re-considered.

In addition the secretaries of each of the touring choirs submitted optimistic reports of increasing the funds collected by their efforts. That week almost £600 *Nipsey Money* was paid out to miner's families.

Despite the increasing success of the choirs the search for support widened with John Potts arranging to address Miners Councils in both Manchester and Durham to ask for assistance.

In the houses owned by Mr Betts, the lay preacher, neither *Eviction Orders* nor *Notices to Quit* had been enforced so the tenants continued to live there rent free. In some cases mothers with children, and indeed whole families who had been evicted from colliery houses, simply moved into those owned by Mr Betts. This situation was not allowed to continue; on Monday of the week ending the 2nd of September the tenants were formally notified:

'All who had not left the houses by today week would have to appear and show cause at Pontefract West Riding Court.'

During the week ending the 9th of September:

'A posse of police from Pontefract District, were marshalled in front of Hemsworth Police Station and marched down to Kinsley under Inspectors Dykes and Hartley to continue evictions.'

The evictions were fairly uneventful until the police reached Gorton Street and the house of Bob Battye, miner and musician:

'As the policemen started to carry out belongings, Bob and his son entertained the crowd by playing the concertina and harp.'

Whilst the police emptied the house next to Bob's they played *Selling up His Happy Home,* as they finished and left, *Dead March in Saul,* and when one of the policemen entered his house, *See the Conquering Hero Comes.* As more police entered the house Bob and his son left; while a neighbour shielded the harp with an umbrella the pair played a lively cakewalk whilst the women and children did a jig. Seeing his belongings put in the street proved too much for Bob, with tears rolling down his cheeks he played *Home Sweet Home* with the people around singing the words to his music.... As Bob was overcome with sadness one man cried: *'Cheer up Bob and don't be silly',* one or two retorted angrily:

'It's all reight thee talking like that. Thee wait till tha has to go through wi it an then tha'll know abaht it.'

Drying his eyes Bob played for another 20 minutes, when he finished he passed his cap among the policemen; one constable did put something in it which was a signal for a shower of coppers from the crowd. The musicians bowed their heads in thanks, then played their finale which included: *Death of Nelson, Hiawatha* and *Where is Now the Merry Old Party.* The final song was accompanied by the singing of the assembled onlookers.

For that brief moment Bob Battye's impromptu concert brought a cheerful note to the dreadful proceedings. This safety-valve of using sarcastic humour in the face of adversity was demonstrated at the house two doors further up the row from Bob's: *Beware of the Dog* had been chalked on the walls signifying the presence of a little India rubber dog. On another house further up the same street was written *Beware of Black-Clocks.* The choir touring the Mexborough district returned to the village on Tuesday unable to raise sufficient

A Gentle EVICTION
New STREET Kinsley

donations to justify the funds needed to continue their travels. In the township itself neighbours and friends continued to rally support: Mr George Hillier of the Kinsley Mission had obtained two caravans to house two of the families evicted during the week and the children now being housed and fed by the Elstone family numbered fifty three.

The dispute appeared to present a dilemma for the Reverend Gilbert of Hemsworth Parish Church who advised his flock:

'It is extremely difficult at a juncture of this kind to suggest what should be our course of action as Christian people. It is impossible, or nearly so, for an outsider to do anything without seeming to take a part for one side or the other, and this we need not say ought to be avoided as far as possible.'

On Wednesday during the Trades Union Congress being held at Hanley, the President, James Sexton, announced receipt of a telegram stating there had been more evictions at Hemsworth that day when a further 70 families had been made homeless. Mr W. Morgan representing the Welsh Miners moved a resolution condemning the Colliery Owners for evicting women and children and then proposed a collection for the sufferers' which was unanimously adopted by Congress.

On Saturday the 9th of September Mr Burniston, solicitor, applied for and was granted a further 70 *Ejectment Orders* to be carried out in 21 days time against tenants in *Betts' Houses* in Bond Street and New Street, Kinsley. The local newspaper carried an almost idyllic report, describing the camp as being '*Nice and Peaceful.'* Its tranquillity being happily broken at the end of the school day as:

'Bands of children armed with sticks and cans could be seen every day gathering a harvest of Blackberries and Elderberries from hedges in the lane, others gathered herbs of various kinds. The women in the camp took it in turns to wash clothes in a newly erected Boiling Copper which appeared to be always on the go.'

Evicted household
at Kinsley
Oct. 3/05
Wales, photo:
Parrot. The Lodger
45

Prior to the advent of television and radio entertainment was live and local, in the tented village it comprised mainly of meeting together and sing-alongs.

A growing politicisation starts to become apparent with speakers such as Phillip Snowden and Miss Ford the prominent I.L.P member from Leeds, visiting the camp accompanied by a Miss Peddle, a singer from the U.S.A. Miss Peddle entertained the children by singing American Negro songs and distributing sweets and in the evening Mr Snowden and Miss Ford gave talks on using their votes intelligently.

As mentioned earlier, Hemsworth colliery workers living in Hemsworth Town and the nearby village of Ackworth began to show resentment towards the residents of Kinsley, who they felt were receiving more than their share of aid from the Miners Committee. Some of the heat was taken out of the situation by the Reverend Gilbert who:

'Has been enabled to give a substantial breakfast every morning to around 56 children in the Parish Hall.'

In an effort to boost collections the strike committee changed tactics sending a choir of 12 boys, escorted by Joe Holland and John Marks, to Thurnscoe and Goldthorpe. In a similar vein miners from the Kinsley pit living in the village of Ackworth sent a choir of 12 male singers to the villages surrounding Leeds. Even from this distant perspective it is heart warming to read that when this group sang in Kippax:

'The choir had the assistance of 300 school children of the village who marched around the district singing and collecting in aid of the Hemsworth Relief Fund.'

These efforts allowed the committee to spend £80 on the purchase of children's boots and shoes as well as paying out 2 shillings *Nipsey Money* to each miner.

The efforts of the Relief Committee in appealing to the Trades Groups were monumental in securing aid for their colleagues from every available source. Collecting sheets were placed at Doncaster Races with a reminder: *'Not to Forget the Evicted at Hemsworth.'* These appeals were augmented by a large parcel of clothing from *The Yorkshire Factory Times* and two hundredweight of fish from a *'friend in Hull.'*

Whilst the miners continued to raise money to feed their families the Colliery Company struggled to reduce its overheads. To this end an appeal was lodged against the level of rates levied on the colliery. Their pleas to the assessment committee for relief failed and at the beginning of September 1905 an order for payment of unpaid rates was issued though payment was again delayed as the company took its case to the next level of authority.

On Thursday the 18th of October the West Riding Quarter Sessions met to hear the appeal. The company's solicitor claimed:

'They were appealing against the assessment of £8,000. With respect to the Hemsworth collieries their contention was that this sum should be reduced to a vanishing point.

The company was formed in December 1903, at present their affairs were in the hands of a receiver for the debenture holders. In considering what the assessment ought to be, they must look at the questions which would be put by a hypothetical tenant. In pursuing enquiries they would find that the collieries were surrounded more or less closely, by 4 other collieries: South Kirkby, Monkton, Acton Hall and Featherstone, and that at Hemsworth a tenant would have to pay an increased price of ¼ per ton for getting the coal, as compared to the others.'

Chairman: *"Is there a reason for that?"*

Mr Shepherd: *"The only reason is that the company was formed and the price fixed in a boom year."*

Chairman: *"Does that not affect the other collieries?"*

Mr Shepherd: *"For some reason or other they were working at ¼ per ton less. During the year ending 1904 the coal sales amounted to 429,283 tons and that realised £161,582-14s-10d. Total working expenses deducting machinery, expenses, repairs and depreciation amounted to £166,838-1s-6d, and thus on the gross receipts there was a loss of over £5,000. Going into the question of other reductions, the capital required to work the concern was £20,000 which he considered to be reasonable for such an undertaking.*

The total interest on that for deduction purposes he put at 13% and this comes to £2,500.

Thus before they get anywhere near the rateable value they must deduct the loss of £5,253 on the gross receipts and the £7,500 interest on capital, as well as repairs £1,412 and depreciation £1,500. They were thus left with an adverse balance of £15,667.

Was it likely that a tenant would pay £8,000 for the privilige (sic) of making a loss of £15,000. There were other factors involved, the Shafton Seam which was exhausted in April this year produced 9,708 tons from the beginning of the year until it closed and the loss on it was £2,790. The Barnsley Seam had not been worked at all this year, and in keeping it in working order a loss of £432 had been incurred. The Haigh Moor Seam was worked until August when the dispute caused it to be closed. The tonnage from January 1st until then was 95,850 and the loss was £2,105.

Thus the position now was much worse than in 1904. One seam was worked out, another had no commercial value, and the third was unworkable because of the strike."

In his evidence, James Creer, Secretary of the Company which owned the lease of the coalfields, claimed:

'On the price list awarded by the Arbitrator who was appointed some time ago, it was impossible to work the collieries. If the price list could be settled so as to allow a profit, the collieries would be re-opened, but more capital would be required in order to raise the tonnage, anticipated at 2,500 a day when the company was formed.'

Mr Ellison for the respondents pointed out:

"The objection against the rating assessment was based on a misconception of the Colliery Company. If the pits were occupied as pits it was immaterial whether a profit was made or not. If the colliery had been worked out and altogether abandoned the case would be different. However no evidence had been given to show that the colliery had been exhausted. On the contrary they had a statement that 'Given a price-list which suited the company, and more capital they could raise 2500 tons a day.' The company had even sent a certificate for their tonnage for 1906 with a view to a statement being made.

He agreed that according to the Principles of Rating the procedure used to assess collieries and railways appeared to be wrong. However it was a procedure agreed by both industries and used by them for over 20 years. Indeed it 'had been recognised by Judges in the Law Courts as the most convenient way to rate collieries' and it was always the method adopted."

At the conclusion of the hearing the appeal was dismissed. Having been unsuccessful in both appeals a final order for payment was issued.

In a display of support for the Hemsworth miners the Labour Council, Normanton and District Trades Council, the I.L.P. and other societies organised a demonstration at How Hill Park. In spite of the heavy rain the large crowd remained around to hear John Potts deliver a blistering attack on the Coal Owners, explaining:

'The men were fighting to defend the principle of arbitration.' He believed *'the Hemsworth Colliery Company was being backed up in what they had done by the Coal Owners Association.'*

In a final criticism Potts drew attention to the fact that the colliery company put its 100 ponies into the hands of two farmers who were given instructions:

'The horses are to be well cared for, this proves the company cares more for their horses than for human beings who have been turned out on the streets.'

In support of the Hemsworth miners the chairman, John Nolan, informed the crowd that the union branches he represented (Altofts No. 1 & No. 2):

'Had decided on a levy of 6d per week until some settlement had been arrived at.'

The meeting was ended by a speech from J. Garbutt of Hemsworth who praised the Umpire, then *'advocated shooting the magistrates who issued the eviction orders.'* Ending his contribution to great applause with the cry:

'It is no wonder the people hear the cry of the Israelites of old O Lord. O Lord how long are we going to suffer.'

Collections at the meeting raised £9-5s-6d, other donations from men at Pope and Pearson's Colliery £3 plus £1 from the Amalgamated Society of Engineers.

A further 70 evictions were planned for the following week. In anticipation of these many families had found alternative accommodation leaving 24 to be billeted in tents.

The Kinsley Hotel already housing 54 children managed to house a further 6 children bringing their total to 60. Again planning for the worst the committee appealed to The West Riding Education Committee who agreed:

'That the relief committee be allowed the use of the intended school for 10/- a week as sleeping accommodation for the children.'

On Thursday of the week ending the 30th of September a gift of ½ a beast, approximately 23/24 stones in weight, was given for distribution throughout the Township. The meat was cut into three pieces and distributed to the Victoria Club for people in Common End and Highfield, to the West End Club and to Kinsley.

On Tuesday the 3rd of October 30 policemen led by Superintendent Hollis assembled; on their arrival at Kinsley Inspector Sykes divided the group into 3 sections to carry out the evictions. As the evictions started some of the Belgians employed on the coke ovens watched with interest. One disgusted onlooker commented:

'An they call England a free country. Turning us Englishmen out of house and home and passing them there Belgiums (sic) ower.'

Once again in the midst of the evictions humour and stoicism in the face of adversity was apparent:

Joe Holland of no. 36 Railway Terrace, known as *Bones* and member of a minstrel band, made the most of the occasion:

'Propped up on the parlour mantle piece was a small stuffed policeman and near it a gaudy tissue paper black minstrel was set up on a large stick. These guys were laughingly carried out by the first constable, then all ten constables lined up (with effigies held on high) to have their photographs taken.'

Kinsley Evictions
Oct 3/05
34

The corner house in King Street was home to a family who augmented their income by selling fish and chips:

'The woman of the house seemed bent on having fun at the police's expense. When her cooking stove, covered in grease, was brought out by policemen she brought out her bright tin and brass pan. Asking the photographer to 'wait a minute' she undid her hairpins, quickly re-arranged her coiffure and discarded her shawl. After an injunction to the policeman to watch the 'dicky bird' she allowed her photograph to be taken, amidst a great deal of laughing and cries of 'e's gotten thi'. In the house next door the crowd watched in amusement as a 'young woman wanted her photo taken (at her bedroom window) but she wanted to hold a bundle of bedding which a stalwart young man in blue was lowering out of the window.' He was clearly of the opposite opinion, whilst they gently struggled in the open window, the bundle dropped. But not before the couple had been snapped. The young woman then drew a laugh from the crowd by pretending to photograph them with a child's Magic Lantern and by a few sparring matches with the police.'

As the storm clouds darkened the sky a company of workmen under the charge of the Relief Committee loaded drays and barrows to cart the evictee's furniture to the designated storage areas, whilst others erected a further 24 tents to house the latest arrivals. By 3 o'clock the rain fell in torrents with only 30 out of the 64 warrants served.

Within the village the profile of the I.L.P. was increased with a *Clarion Van* being used to house one evicted family. Almost every working mans club in the area had set up a *Soup Kitchen* to ensure families received at least one meal every day. Offers to house and feed children of the village for the duration of the strike were received from supporters in Bolton, Leicester, Leeds and Bradford.

The following week two events had a direct impact on the participants:

On the 7th of October it was reported:

'The Fitzwilliam Hemsworth Colliery Company's affairs are in liquidation, with a view it is said, to the reconstruction of the company.'

At the Miners Federation conference held in Blackpool, following strong criticism of the Hemsworth Coal Owner's actions, conference passed a resolution allocating £1,000 for the erection of dwellings for the families of the evicted miners.

Kier Hardie, Leader of the Independent Labour party, visited the township on Saturday the 15th of October. Addressing the assembled mass of villagers from an open window on the second floor of the Kinsley Hotel, Hardie referred to the problems the miners encountered trying to get assistance from the Board of Guardians:

'The Local Government Board laid it down clearly, whether or not blame or responsibility attached to the parents, the Guardians were defying the law by their present actions.'

His examination of the colliery houses in Kinsley showed they were:

'The worst he had ever seen', his solution was *'...the County Council ought to own the houses then there would be no more evictions in the case of strikes or lock outs......'*

Turning his attention to the Yorkshire Miners Association he stated:

'The leaders of the Y.M.A. might give more help than they had.'

His speech ended with a rallying cry to the miners that:

'At the next General Election, whether Roman Catholic or Protestant, stand shoulder to shoulder and try to put a labour member in.'

In his speech of thanks, Potts who had been a staunch Liberal supporter during the notorious by-election in Barnsley when the miners stoned Pete Curran the Socialist Candidate, outlined the change in his own political beliefs:

'I once went against Mr Hardie and his policy but my views have changed and were Kier Hardie or any other Labour man to stand for that constituency at the next election, he would have his support.'

In Horbury the local Brass Band led a successful demonstration in aid of the locked out miners and their families. The demonstration which culminated in a meeting addressed by John Potts and M. Gibson from Wakefield raised additional funds for the relief committee:

Total Raised.	*£13-14s-2½d*
Expenses, Printing, Postage.	*£1-6s-2½d*
Refreshments for Visitors.	*£1-6s-2½d*
Amount to Fund.	*£11-18s-0d*

Whilst most of the miners and their families stayed on the right side of the law the Wakefield Express reported on a court case involving two youngsters:

'Two Hemsworth schoolboys, Harold Hancock aged 12 and Thomas Vaughan aged 9, were charged at Pontefract Court on Saturday with stealing 4 slices of Bread and Dripping.'

The boys were given a *Caution,* their parents however had to pay 9 shillings costs.

The Miners Federation decided to use the T.U.C. grant of £1,000 to obtain leases on Mr Betts houses in Kinsley. Recent memories of Betts' behaviour caused great resentment in the camp mainly because:

'They did not want to go back into houses owned by Mr Betts, as he had not behaved in a proper manner towards them.'

AFTER THE KINSLEY EVICTIONS

However the freezing cold winds, heavy rain and bitter frost that hit the township that weekend persuaded the majority that the comfort of a warm fireside, even in Betts' houses, was better than the prospect of being snowed up and freezing in their tents during winter.

Once made, the decision was quickly implemented:

'People began to flit on Monday, by 10 o'clock Tuesday morning there was not a tent to be seen, the ground looked deserted and rather singular.'

A demonstration was held in the campsite the following Sunday afternoon. Speakers that day included Kier Hardie, Isabella Ford and Miss McArthur, Secretary of the Ladies Trade Union League, with John Potts presiding. I have included John Potts' opening address mainly because I believe it is a visible milestone in his political journey and an expression of the increasing dissatisfaction with the miner's political representation:

'The Miners Federation was not as he would like to see it either in strength or finances.

He would like to see a National Federation of Miners brought about whereby a man could be elected for Parliament who would put forward the case of the miners in times of trouble, and whoever might be selected should be able to voice the feelings and sentiments and enforce the opinions of the whole of the miners of the United Kingdom. If that were done the position of the miners would not be what it was today. Wages would rise, and conditions would be more advantageous to the workers than those at present existing. Speaking of the leaders of the Yorkshire Miners Association, Mr Potts said that whilst he had great respect for them, and from the outside he was always willing to defend them when unfairly attacked, they were not so energetic as they ought to be, and he hoped and trusted that ere long they wake up and meet the miners in the same resolute manner as they had done aforetimes. He also found want with their action recently when taking a vote as to whether the Miners of Yorkshire be affiliated with the Trades Association. He thought they had taken the wrong step, and he advised the miners of Yorkshire not to let the matter rest until the Y.M.A. was affiliated with all other trades in the country, and by this means they would be much stronger and able to defend against attacks of Employers. He had been identified with the Liberal Party for 20 years, and after this experience he had decided not to use his influence for a candidate who did not come with a straight Labour ticket and he hoped the Yorkshire Miners would vote the same way and call upon any candidate to withdraw who did not go straight from Labour. He also complained strongly of the fact, that although there was such an institution as the Yorkshire Miners Association at Barnsley, and although the people had been evicted from their homes and had been obliged to lodge in tents, yet none of the leaders had been to Hemsworth, to see if they could lend a helping hand and alleviate in any way the distress in the neighbourhood.'

Unfortunately the contributions of the other speakers were not reported, however one could assume that they would have been of a similar vein.

After dinner on Wednesday the children living in the Kinsley Hotel returned to their homes. Mr Elstone however continued to give aid to the youngsters:

'With the money left in his relief fund, Mr Elstone has opened a soup kitchen which will dispense soup to all the children in the village for 4 days a week, on the other two Mr J. Morte will be the provider.'

As a result of the offers to provide temporary homes for the miner's children eleven youngsters left the village on Saturday the 15th:

'8 going to Barrow in Furness, 1 to Leeds, 1 to Cardiff, and 1 to Oldham. An un-named lady is coming from Barrow in Furness today to take boys/girls back with her.'

For the third Tuesday in a row *Ejectment Orders* were enforced with Inspector Hartley leading a dozen policemen to carry out a further eight. These evictions were probably less traumatic than the previous ones as the evicted merely moved their possessions out of one house into one of *Betts' Houses* which had been leased to the Miners Federation.

As before humour and pathos accompanied the evictions:

'One pitiable case was that of an old couple over 70 years of age and the husband tottering about on two sticks. The man who is now unable to work is said to have spent all his life at the colliery and then be turned out in such a heartless way.'

On the lighter side, the removal of a ramshackle hen-hut from a house in Outgang Terrace amused the crowd as the endeavours of the police:

'To keep the structure from tumbling to pieces were really laughable. The crowd were highly delighted with the scene and speedily made way for photographers who were present to snap shot the men in blue in as ridiculous a position as possible. The hen-hut had to be carried for approximately 20 or 30 yards and at every step two or three pieces of rotten timber fell off, and a cheer went up, and a cheer went up when it dropped over a low boundary wall and fell flat.'

Once again the focus for the choirs changed with two choirs being despatched to Manchester and Sheffield, in addition collectors toured Leeds and Bradford areas visiting all *'big works and factories'*. Income to the relief fund for this week exceeded £40 which enabled the

HEMSWORTH LOCK OUT MINERS CHILDREN GOING TO THEIR ADOPTED HOMES

purchase of 300 pairs of children's boots. Messrs Marshall and Co, cap makers, sent approximately 60 children's caps; one for all the children who had lived in the Kinsley Hotel.

An interesting development took place when it was reported:

'A Wakefield man had agreed to supply 2 Bioscopes of a very expensive nature to Mr Potts and a total outlay of £400 with which to tour the country. He had also offered to find four men to play the piano and manipulate the Lanterns. Mr Potts has to find 6 men including himself and form two companies with which to tour the country. There will be 4000 different views including a number of cinematograph films and the slide set will include a large number of pictures of the evictions and the camp. Mr Potts will make an appeal during the interval. It is hoped that a healthy sum will be received each week.'

Unfortunately I have been unable to locate this equipment or these films.

Chapter Five

November 1905 – Land Grabbing

A meeting of the West Yorkshire Coal Owners and Workmen's Joint Board was held on the first Tuesday of November 1905, at which a Conciliation Board of West Yorkshire comprising four representatives from each side (union and owners) agreed:

'*To investigate the merits of the long-standing dispute at the Fitzwilliam and Hemsworth Collieries, and try to find a basis for settlement.*'

The following Tuesday His honour Mr Justice Raikes K.C. heard an application for compensation against the Hemsworth Colliery Company. The applicant, Mr Haverhand:

'*Wished to know whether the company was insured for accidents, and if not whether his claim should be a first charge upon the colliery's estate as this man should be in a better position than an ordinary creditor.*'

The company's solicitor claimed:

'The company was not insolvent, the receiver is in possession and the debenture holders will no doubt lose. Today there is an application in London asking for a stay of all proceedings against the company.'

An order was subsequently made for 18 shillings and 9 pence.

The politicisation of the Hemsworth branch in general, and John Potts in particular, is further evidenced by his open letter to voters in the Normanton By-election:

'He and Mr Bull hoped that the electors of Normanton would insist upon any candidate, whether chosen from the Yorkshire Miners Association, or from any other Trade Union Body, contesting the election on a straight Labour Ticket otherwise we would advise the electorate of Normanton to stick to their rights of selecting a candidate to contest the division.'

Nothing much appears to have been done to break the deadlock between workers and employer, nevertheless support continued to grow, indeed at the beginning of December it was reported:

'On Sunday afternoon a large crowd led by Grange Moor Colliery band followed by bands from Park hill and Sharlston Collieries, marched through Wakefield to the Hippodrome, where a well attended meeting took place.'

Mr Davis, checkwieghman at West Sharlston pit, proposed:

'That this meeting organised by the Wakefield Trades Council strongly protests against the barbarous and cruel treatment inflicted on the miners, their wives and children, by the Fitzwilliam Hemsworth Colliery Owners in the recent evictions, and pledges itself to use every means to render impossible people being forced from their homes in any future industrial dispute.'

Afterwards Ben Turner, parliamentary candidate for Dewsbury, made a passionate speech supporting the resolution which was enthusiastically accepted by the crowd.

Following the speeches some £27 plus 5 parcels of clothing had been donated. In the same week a donation of £10 was received from the Nottingham Miners Association to help feed children affected by the strike. The following Thursday the soup kitchen at the Kinsley Hotel closed due to lack of funding with Mr Elstone passing management of the soup kitchen, including the use of his boiling copper, to the Kinsley Children's Relief Fund Committee. The last of the 400 stones of flour donated by the Halifax Flour Company was distributed on Saturday with 60 stones going to Hemsworth and 40 stones to Kinsley.

John Potts claimed to have received correspondence from the debenture holders of the Company asking for information and demanding confidentiality, of this he stated:

'If this is given there will be strange developments in the Hemsworth dispute.'

According to the newspaper Mr Potts was debarred from giving any more details.

Whilst efforts continued to obtain and keep the public's support, working class politics became increasingly important for the miners in general and the Hemsworth miners in particular, with the Independent Labour Party winning hearts and minds in the mining and industrial communities.

Having received a final refusal from the Hemsworth Board of Guardians to give miners a loan to help them feed their children, Mr Potts said:

'The correspondence will provide splendid electioneering material in

opposition to the Leeds Conservatives at the now fast approaching General Election.'

In recognition of his efforts during the dispute Isaac Burns was elected Chairman of the Hemsworth Education Sub-Committee, in the same week the Co-op Wholesale Society donated £250 to aid miners in Hemsworth and Thrybergh Hall, a further £30 was received from miners in Wales.

On the opposite side of the tracks Richard Fosdick, Managing Director of the Colliery Company, was now fighting for his survival as M.D. of the colliery. In the Chancery Division on Saturday the 2nd of December:

'In the action Fosdick Vs The Fitzwilliam Hemsworth Colliery's Ltd, Mr Justice Joyce had before him a motion for judgement in a debenture holder's action.... The debenture stock was issued under a Trust Deed. His Lordship made the usual order, declaring that the trusts of the deed are to be carried into execution and directing the usual accounts and enquiries.'

To celebrate Christmas the Kinsley Children's Relief Committee planned a treat for the children of the miners from Hemsworth, Kinsley, Ackworth and Featherstone. The joy of this was attenuated by Mr Picken, the Secretary of the Ackworth Relief Fund, who informed members:

'The Soup Kitchen will stop shortly unless assistance is given.'

Whilst the Y.M.A. dealt with issues in Hemsworth and Thrybergh Hall, membership of the Yorkshire Miners Association had fallen by approximately 10,000 since 1900. In an attempt to stem the exodus Y.M.A. officers John Wadsworth and Fred Hall began urging branches to *'bring these people back into the fold.'* Whilst endeavouring to recruit more members the Y.M.A. re-affirmed their support for Joe

Walton, the Liberal Party parliamentary candidate. On the 18th of December, the issue of Y.M.A. official support for the Liberal candidate was discussed at a special meeting of the Hemsworth Miner's Union Branch. The branch agreed to submit the following resolution to the Y.M.A. Secretary at Barnsley for consideration at Council:

'The Hemsworth Branch (Y.M.A.) strongly favours Mr Herbert Smith as candidate in the Labour interest inasmuch as he ran so close with Mr Fred Hall in the selection of the candidate in the recent Normanton By-election. In the event of the Y.M.A. not putting forward a candidate as requested, negotiations are in progress whereby another candidate will be brought out in the interests of Labour, and in opposition to a Tory or to Mr Walton.' The article continued: *'The miner's local leaders at Hemsworth state: They cannot understand why the leaders of the Y.M.A so determinedly oppose a Labour Candidate being run instead of Mr Walton, and fail to assert their independence.'*

On Friday of the same week a large room of Hemsworth Council School was packed with an enthusiastic company of miners presided over by The Reverend Joseph Parkin. The Rev. Parkin set the tone of the meeting in his opening address:

'The 1895 election was fought and won on Beer, the 1900 on Blood, but the 1905 would be fought on The People's Food, the People's Conscience and the question of Chinese Slavery in South Africa. A change was coming now and they as radicals were longing for the fight.'

After his speech Joe Walton took questions from the floor, Potts was again on his feet:

'If workmen are to receive a pension, say at 65 years of age, what percentage would be affected, and of what practical use would it be?'

Mr Walton replied: '*He hoped they would get rid of the antiquated ideas of 'Joe' and start with the matter afresh. He thought it ought to be before 65. In the House with a man like John Burns (loud cheers and cries of Honest John) at the head of the Local Government Board, the first direct representation of Labour in the cabinet, they had much to expect. They would make headway now whereas under the old fossil Gerald Balfour, they got no forrader.'(sic)*

Mr Walton then went on to explain he was in favour of women's suffrage.

The meetings attention focused harshly on Fred Hall of the Y.M.A. who boldly asserted:

'The Labour policy was to smash up Trade Unionism.' In response to expressions of disbelief from the crowd he added:

'The Labour Party when they first set out tried to capture Trade Unions and Co-operative Societies for their own ends.'

Fred Hall's comments sparked a heated debate between Walton and Hall on one side and Isaac Burns, Potts, Bull, and Goddard on the other.

The ripples caused by Fred Hall's remarks which had been reported by local newspapers, spread beyond Hemsworth. The following letter from J. Coutts, Secretary of the I.L.P branch at Normanton was representative of the feeling of anger caused by Fred Hall's remarks:

'Sir
Your issue of last week contained a report of a meeting in support of the canditature, (sic) of Mr Walton at Hemsworth. Mr F. Hall makes the statement that the Labour Party's policy was to Smash up Trades Unionism. Is Mr Hall prepared to withdraw that statement as being delivered in the heat of the moment—a circumstance which often happens during political warfare? If he is not prepared to withdraw,

I challenge Mr Hall to prove it—If he will not prove this statement, the Labour Party will treat it as a base and deliberate fabrication.'

During this time antagonism between the Trade Union hierarchy and newly emerged labourist political groups such as the I.L.P. became fairly vitriolic. In particular the antagonism between the Trade Union Leaders and Victor Grayson, a young militant I.L.P member who contested and won a Parliamentary Seat in the by-election at Colne Valley in 1907, and gave as the three reasons for his victory:

'First because they were worried about what they saw as the Dead Hand of Labour.

Secondly they were increasingly unhappy about the displays of deference being shown by party leaders in parliament.

Thirdly, they were concerned about constraints arising from the apparent electoral understanding between Labour and the Liberals. This expressed itself in their demand to contest Liberal-held seats as a matter of urgency.'

On January the 6th the Hemsworth miners committee received a telegram from the joint committee appointed to look into the Hemsworth dispute, asking them to send 3 delegates to meet the committee at Leeds the following day. Whilst agreeing to send the delegates the committee did not have high hopes of a settlement being reached.

During the following weeks the media's attention was focused on two new developments: The first was a prosecution brought by Potts and Bull on behalf of the Hemsworth miner's branch against two of its members, Messrs W. Lincoln and Daniel Concannon who were accused of stealing £8-7s-3d from the money collected for the locked-out miners. After a 6 hour legal wrangle in Pontefract Magistrates Court the chairman of the bench concluded:

'There was no case to go before a jury.'

Secondly, this decision which angered the Hemsworth officers was, they claimed, as a result of officials of the Y.M.A:

'Sending into that Court of Law, a Lawyer, who prevented figures supplied from this office (Y.M.A. Offices) *being put to court to prove the case. Is that manly, is it straight; and the case failed. It might have told another tale but for that action.'*

Unwilling to let the matter be forgotten, Potts and Bull with the approval of their union branch decided:

'The facts of the case are to be placed before the miners of Yorkshire and the General Public, through the public press and by Circular, so that everyone may judge as to the decision of the magistrates.'

For the next five weeks the local newspaper carried an exchange of letters giving opinions, accusations and counter accusations from Potts, Bull, Lincoln and Concannon. These were added to by someone, or some group, using the nom-de-plume *The Spectator* who managed to write regular odes attacking the Hemsworth miners in general and Potts and Bull in particular. In an attempt to put the record straight, Joe Barnsley of Hemsworth had a letter published outlining the root of the problem and the attempt to find a solution. The basis of the branch's action is contained in this letter.

'Because of dissatisfaction with regard to the Nipsey Fund, so manipulated by Concannon and Lincoln, the men of Hemsworth colliery instructed Potts to examine the accounts and report thereon, and called attention to some discrepancies in these accounts. Concannon and Lincoln were called upon to give an explanation, but could give no satisfactory explanation. After discussing the case at various meetings Lincoln and Concannon asked to be allowed to put their case to a Chartered Accountant, to which the

men readily consented and agreed to pay the cost. At a subsequent Nipsey meeting Concannon stated he was prepared to put his case. There being insufficient time to discuss the case satisfactorily at this meeting the men fixed a meeting for 10 o'clock next day, especially to deal with the case. This meeting was duly held, but Lincoln did not attend and Concannon, although an hour late put in an appearance. He told the men that he and Lincoln had not been to a Chartered Accountant, neither had they done anything, and asked for another week in which to put his case. Another week was conceded by the men. Finally at a meeting (Sept 6th 1905) the case was still unsettled. Potts suggested that both sides should submit their figures to Mr John Hoskin, who should decide, and any balance proven to be due Concannon and Lincoln should refund. Lincoln said they preferred to be prosecuted. The men accepted the challenge, and passed a resolution to prosecute (Sept 22nd 1905). The men appointed Potts and Bull to carry out their wishes with regard to the prosecution of Lincoln and Concannon. Thus it is plain to any fair-minded person that in prosecuting Lincoln and Concannon, Potts and Bull were simply doing the bidding of the men.'

This incident widened the schism between the differing political groups of miners in the Yorkshire Miners Association which culminated in the Corton Wood branch tabling a resolution to the Association demanding the expulsion of Potts and Bull from the Union.

In response to this further attack on Potts and Bull the Hemsworth branch met on the Monday evening to discuss the officers of the Y.M.A. *Victimising* John Potts.

Once again the:

'Men declared themselves to be unanimously in favour of John Potts and passed a vote of confidence in him. Thanking him for his past work and pledging themselves to support him in his politics.'

The branch committee's actions were reinforced the following evening at a well attended meeting in the Kinsley Hotel, during which a resolution was passed:

'Appointing Messrs Potts and Bull to draw up a circular of facts, to be placed before the miners in the County, and, to attend branches of the Y.M.A and lay before them the true facts of the case.'

Having obtained the full support of his branch members Potts responded aggressively to this attack by visiting all the union branches in the area, explaining his case, dealing with their questions and asking for their support in his fight against the action to have him thrown out of the union. In conjunction with these personal appeals Potts had the following letter published in the Wakefield Express:

'Sir
Permit me space for a few observations relative to the famous Corton Wood resolution to the last Yorkshire Miners Association Council, seeking to introduce into the association the principle of victimising its own members who dare to publicly express their political and private opinions. Have our Corton Wood fellow trade unionists realised the terrible weapon for argument they would thereby place at the discretion of the employers when charged by the Y.M.A. with victim making of miners who dare to stand up for their trade union principles. Will the Corton Wood Secretary and the Y.M.A. authority answer the following questions?

1) *Were Corton-Wood miners, by ordinary meeting, consulted upon their famous suggested resolution prior to introduction to Council and how many members had a voice therein?*

2) *Did the resolution emanate from the rank and file or, was it engineered for Council?*

3) *Upon what grounds was such resolution drawn?*

4) *Under what rule did the Y.M.A. officials place upon the minutes an attack on my private political opinion?*

5) *Did Mr Walsh a would-be official well known for his disorganised branch compare me to a Howden of Denaby?*

6) *Did a delegate state in council, as reported to our committee, that they ought to get without me while they had a chance?*

Potts went on to defend the I.L.P. even though he was not a member of this party, he:

'Would not feel himself lowered in dignity if he was.'

His letter ended with a direct challenge to the Secretary of the Corton Wood Branch:

'If Mr Walsh will call a large meeting of his men in the South Kirkby Board Schools we will meet him from the Hemsworth branch, not only to discuss my letter, but also to discuss the recent action against the Hemsworth miners.'

The actions of Mr Walsh upset Hemsworth people working at South Kirkby Colliery so much that one of their ranks, namely Isaac burns, issued a circular challenging Walsh and his position:

'An Open Reply and Challenge to Mr Walsh

I challenge him to let the men declare by Ballot in whom they have the most confidence, the one receiving the largest number of votes to stay on and work for the workers, the unsuccessful one to take it as a vote of no-confidence and seek work elsewhere.'

Ike Burns continued his attacks on Walsh and Roberts, claiming that between £10 and £12 a week *Nipsey Money* had been collected from South Kirkby miners:

'Then Messrs Walsh and Roberts took up a collection, presumably for the relief of Little Ones, yet, without any authority whatever, they handed the whole collection to an entirely different fund. The men who had paid the Nipsey Money were indignant, and they swear they will not pay another halfpenny while such men have the handling of the money. And in proof of their statement we have unfortunately to release record that last week's collection only realised 3/11d, what a drop from £12 odd.'

It is interesting to note that there appears to have been no recorded response from Walsh or Roberts to these attacks and challenges.

On the 24th of February it was reported that a meeting of over 1000 miners was held in the Hemsworth Council School to receive a report of the Y.M.A. deputation which had been appointed to meet the committee representing the interests of the Colliery Company. The deputation consisting of Herbert Smith, S. Jacks, J. Hoskin and G. H. Hirst explained they had met about 16 times but all their efforts had come to nothing. They now asked for a free hand to approach the official receiver to see if an arrangement could be made with him to get the pits re-started. Unfortunately nothing positive was to come from their endeavours.

There is a gap in the newspaper records between March and July 1906; it seems the Hemsworth Express was discontinued, its role being filled by the Wakefield Express.

Optimism was high in the village at the beginning of July when it was reported that Major Shaw accompanied by John Shaw, owner of Featherstone Main and South Kirkby Collieries, visited the Hemsworth Colliery to check on its condition. Speculation on this was confirmed by an article in the Wakefield Express (7th July) which announced:

'We are now able to state that purchase was made Last Monday.'

This news provoked a mixed reaction from people in the Township:

'Tradesmen and shop owners dusted their stock and looked confidently busy as the prospect of good times re-emerged. On the other hand the miners merely asked, how will this affect us?'

The local miner's branch split into two distinct factions: one faction:

'Disbelieved the report of the purchase and also, that if a purchase had been made they would not negotiate for a settlement. They intended to stick to the price list award given by Mr Atkinson at the start of the dispute.'

The opposing camp was reported as:

'being very indignant at the attitude taken by their colleagues, in so publicly making the men appear not to be in favour of negotiations being carried on.'

Another leader speaking as *the man in the street* said the miners were prepared to reason:

'To them it does not matter whether they work for Mr Fosdick for 7/- a day or Major Shaw. They would have preferred Mr Fosdick the Old Master for whom they have a great amount of respect and love, in spite of what had taken place. They really had been living in hope that he would be able to make some settlement.'

In some quarters the sale of the colliery would provide the opportunity to improve the appalling conditions of the miners and their families. In the words of one reporter:

'It is hoped the delay will not be long as the people cannot stick it out much longer on the under-feeding system. One of the most common sights in Hemsworth and, one of the most touching, is to see little children without boots and stockings and their clothes in rags and tatters going (with a sop box barrow) the round of the

houses where the bread winner is known to be working with the pathetic plea: Please can you give us a bit of coil. If it's only a little piece we'd be ever so much obliged. In no case is this request refused and very often a piece of bread or half a loaf or so goes with the little gift of coal.'

As everyone waited for the Y.M.A. and the Shaw family to come to an agreement on terms for the Hemsworth pits, opinions on the start date for the pits was divided. Many held the belief that nothing would be done until the end of November and the abolition of the Coal Tax which would help the industry. Others were hopeful of an early start but not looking forward to the stiff backs and bruised limbs which the first week would entail after such a long lay off.

Collectors were still being dispatched to collect for the *Nipsey Pay-Outs* however it was now costing as much to send the collectors out as they were bringing back to the camp:

'Grants and Donations.	*£62- 6s- 2d*
Collecting Books	*£75- 10s- 4½d*
Collecting expenses inc railway fares.	*£65- 6s- 5½d'*

At the beginning of August a demonstration marking the second anniversary of the strike was held in Hemsworth. Local miners were joined by colleagues from South Kirkby, Ryhill, Snydale, Ackworth, South-Heindley, Grimethorpe, Wombwell and Featherstone Collieries. Led by Bands from Kinsley, South Kirkby and Ackworth, and with banners flying, they paraded through Hemsworth to Common End where a speaker's platform had been erected. In his opening address the Chairman, Isaac Burns, outlined the objectives of the rally:

'1) To raise funds to lessen the suffering of the women and children of Hemsworth miners.

2) To show non-union men the benefits of joining the Y.M.A.

3) To encourage existing union members.'

In his speech Potts gave a breakdown of the *Nipsey Fund*:

'During the past year they had received £9,398-8s-7½d, of this £1,495-9s-2½d had come from the Y.M.A. in grants and by books whilst £7,902-19s-5d had been contributed by the public. The average each week had been £27-15s-0d from miners and £146-7s-0d from outside. The average Nipsey Money paid out had been 1s-9½d per man, per week. But for the last nine or ten weeks they had paid only a shilling per man and last week one and six per man.'

Burns then levelled his criticism at the Y.M.A:

'The miners of Yorkshire were not doing what they should to help the miners at Hemsworth. South Kirkby, their near neighbours are not doing their duty by them. There were too many non-union men there and the men who had charge there ought to set about and organise it in the way it should be organised. ...he doubted if there had been a dozen non-union men over the past 10 years.'

Potts then clarified his branch's position on negotiating with the new owners of the colliery:

'So far as the lying correspondent in a paper published in Castleford was concerned let him give the lie direct to such statements as appeared in the paper. The men were as anxious as any man in Yorkshire to go to work. It didn't matter to them who owned the colliery; they had done fairly well with the old firm. If Mr Shaw is perfectly willing to negotiate we are prepared to meet him tomorrow.... They would accept Mr Shaw's suggestions freely and willingly and had no intention of doing otherwise than bargaining for fair conditions.'

The large crowd were then entertained by speeches from John Sparing of Burnley, John Nolan from Normanton, Joe Walton M.P.

Barnsley and John Guest of South Heindley who appealed for more support for the Hemsworth miners:

'They are fighting this battle and the battle of all other miners in Yorkshire and should be well looked after.'

The grand sum of £12-9s-3½d was raised at the rally which included £10 donated by Joe Walton M.P. This was augmented by Barnsley Co-op who due to lobbying by T. Watmough donated 1200 loaves to be distributed at 200 per week over the next six weeks.

The I.L.P support was unwavering; the meeting room at Kinsley was used every Wednesday evening for small discussion group meetings and the ballroom at the Kinsley Hotel for the larger ones. Speakers at these venues included S. Hartley on *'How to make our Boys and Girls Good citizens'* and J. Robertson, vice president of the Scottish Miners Union, on *'Labour Representation',* and his failure to understand *'Why the Yorkshire Miners leaders pandered to the Liberal party'.*

A few weeks later, one week before a national ballot was held on the topic, J. T. Jones, vice president of the Rhonda Valley miner's federation, spoke: *'On the advantages of the Miners Federation affiliating with the Labour Representation Committee.'*

The issue of *Land Ownership* became the main focus for discussion in the township with a number of meetings being held on topics such as the '*Sacred Rights of Property* and *Land Laws.*' Indeed the text of one lay preacher at the Common End Church Mission Hall, reflecting the views of his congregation was: *'Go Ye and Posses the Land.'*

Inspired by the oratory of a *Socialist Itinerant* called Muck McCutcheon, a group of miner's decided to create a camp and begin to cultivate Brierley Common. They were aware they would be evicted but were determined to draw attention to what they regarded as

Hemsworth Unemployed
Back to the Land
Aug 24/08
A. COOLING

ridiculous land laws. In this they were successful insofar as this issue occupied many column inches in the local newspapers over the next few weeks.

The *Landgrabbers* erected two *Bell Tents* and began to dig and plant vegetables in an area of Brierley Common. A few days later when three Policemen arrived to view proceedings they had cultivated an area 25 yards by 12 yards and planted it with potatoes and cabbages. Despite being advised by the police the land was private and they required the owner's permission to occupy and cultivate it, the group continued their horticultural adventure. The men's action viewed by the establishment as a direct challenge to the sacred *Rights of Property* was vehemently condemned by the local press:

'The crass stupidity of the men who yesterday seized a portion of Brierley Common may be regarded as a piece of midsummer madness. That a body of men supposed to be civilised could be so worked upon by the frenzied oratory of an Itinerant Socialist does not show an overly supply of common sense on their part.'

During the next days as digging continued, some fortification topped by a red flag was erected as a token of defiance. The following Wednesday a bus load of policemen arrived, removed the *Landgrabbers* from the *Common* then charged ten of their ranks with:

'Doing damage to the amount of 18/- to land at Brierley Common ...by digging it with spades.'

Others were charged with aiding and abetting this act. On their appearance in Court William Bull, spokesman for the miners', offered no defence claiming they had not been given enough notice of the trial, and they had not damaged the land but had actually improved it by their efforts. ...His plea fell on stony ground, the miners were fined 2 shillings and 6 pence each and ordered to pay a further 2 shillings

in damages or face 7 days in jail. In an interview after the trial Bull informed reporters:

'Joseph Barnsley and Hugh Hodgkiss had refused to pay the fine and damages and would be removed to Wakefield to serve their term of 7 days.'

Chapter Six

The End of the Strike

Efforts to break the deadlock continued, on Tuesday the 29th of August at the Bull Hotel in Wakefield a private meeting took place between Major Shaw, Percy Greaves, Mr Snow and Mr Archer for the colliery owners, with J. Wadsworth, Fred Hall and Herbert Smith for the Y.M.A., and J. Potts, T. Watmough, M. Smith and Mr Starkey representing the Hemsworth miners. No decision was reached, however both sides agreed to meet again on September the 12th.

At the Macro economic level the general state of the market for coal was mixed: A heat-wave in September reduced demand for house coal which prevented coal owners from raising the price as they normally did at this time of year; their answer was to put colliers on short time. Demand for coal in the manufacturing industry remained steady, with some scarcity in the output of high quality coal keeping the price up. The demand for Gas Coal had showed a slight improvement with several small contracts being completed at prices higher than in previous years. Indeed one colliery had secured a contract, usually won by Westphallian pits, for 45,000 tons for delivery to continental ports.

During the first week of September to help prepare for re-commencement of work at the pit, the new owners wrote to the miner's committee asking for 6 by-workmen to clear the accumulations of dirt and rubbish which had accrued since the stoppage. Wages were to be paid at the rates paid prior to the dispute. This move augmented by the buoyant market for good quality coal and the imminent abolition of the coal tax generated optimism that the meeting between colliery owners and miners, scheduled for the following week, would signal an end to the strike.

Within the Y.M.A. politics were becoming an increasingly bitter area of combat. James Walsh had accepted an invitation from the Attercliffe trade unionists to stand as their candidate in the event of a Parliamentary by-election. In response to this the South Kirkby Y.M.A. branch passed a unanimous resolution protesting against the selection of Mr Walsh by the Attercliffe miners; they supported this action by sending a letter to their Attercliffe colleagues asking them to re-consider their decision. It is interesting to note that Mr Walsh would be opposed by Hy Dews, an I.L.P candidate and a Tory.

Nipsey Fund returns for the week of the 15th of September showed a positive balance of £10 between collecting expenses and money collected; grants totalling £45-6s-2d, including £10 from the Cab Drivers Association, enabled £47-10s-0d to be paid out. In the same week the last of the 1200 loaves from Barnsley Co-op were distributed.

The action demanding the expulsion of Potts and Bull from the Yorkshire Miners Association was coming to a head, with a ballot on the *Dismembering* planned for Friday the 14th of September. Prior to this ballot being taken 500 miners from the Hemsworth branch visited near-by pits handing out leaflets signed by seventeen branch officials stating:

'Five Reasons why Messrs Potts and Bull should not be dismembered.'

A letter from John Potts dated the 13th of September 1906 asking his fellow miners to delay the vote until he had the opportunity to present his side of the story was published in the Wakefield Express:

'Sir
Would you be good enough to insert in the columns of your esteemed paper an appeal to the miners of Yorkshire to waive voting upon dismembering Messrs Potts and Bull, so eagerly desired by the Y.M.A. officials, pending our side of the case being presented being sent out to branches? This matter is being officially rushed to prevent defence and the facts becoming known which will place a different aspect before the miner. The officials seem afraid to waive the question and permit our side being placed before Council as by so doing the true position would be revealed.'

The minutes of the Y.M.A. Council meeting of August reveal:

'That the particulars be printed on the Minutes and the result as to whether Messrs J. Potts and W.O. Bull be dismembered, or otherwise, be sent in to the next Executive Committee. Of the 68 branch delegates who voted, 23 voted for Dismemberment at once, 25 voted for the men attending the Council to explain.'

These minutes also contained the following:

'NOTE.

Gentlemen—An unfortunate incident at the Trades Union Congress was brought about by the conduct of Messrs John Potts and William. O. Bull. They never asked the Yorkshire Miners Association to bring the Hemsworth Case before the Trades Union Congress, but they wrote direct to Mr Steadman, M. P.'

and: *'Secretary or the Trades Union Congress to be allowed to send a deputation to appear before the Congress to put the Hemsworth case and thus would have caused expense to send that deputation had it been allowed. While at the same time, if your Association or Officials had been asked, the case could have been put without any expense whatever, providing the Parliamentary Committee would have agreed to that course. When Messrs Bull and Potts got to Liverpool they then issued a circular as follows:-*

IMPORTANT

The Truth about Hemsworth Stoppage

Gentlemen

Arising upon the statement made by Mr Fred Hall, M.P. to the Congress at Tuesday's sitting, we wish to draw the Delegate's attention to the following facts:

1.) That the Hemsworth Colliery employers refused to abide by the Umpire's Award ever since that Award was made.

2.) That we had to immediately resort to County Court actions in order to enforce the workmen's dues under that Award, and cases were so fought and won.

3.) For over twelve months Mr Fred Hall has had in his possession a tabulate statement of workmen's cases dealing with the employer's refusal to the Arbitration Award. The monies are owing to the men today. Such statement was officially asked for by the Y.M.A. leaders and supplied by the Hemsworth local branch. The cases date back to the time of taking up the award.

4) The poor locked out men, large numbers of whom have been denied the Right To Work for over two years, have never been against any further attempts to arrive at a just settlement outside that award, which cost our society hundreds of pounds to secure (although we submit such award ought to be by all means enforced). We are further of opinion that our officials ought to take off their jackets and with firm determination fight for its maintenance.

Friends assist your fellow Trade Unionists of Hemsworth who are nobly fighting in defence of the Principle of Arbitration

We are Gentlemen
JOHN POTTS, Branch Secretary
Wm. O. BULL

P.S: – We are delegated to seek permission to state our case to Congress.

You will note they say at the bottom: We are delegated to seek permission to state our case to congress, while the Hemsworth delegate at our council meeting stated that these two men were not delegated by the Hemsworth branch to attend the Trade Union Congress at Liverpool, and these two men, in our opinion, are doing the Hemsworth case a great and serious injury. Let it be clearly understood, that if these two men had not interfered and made it impossible to put the matter before Congress, the Officials would have undoubtedly seen the Parliamentary Committee and put the case, not only of Hemsworth, but Thrybergh Hall and other men who are suffering at present in Yorkshire, and would have secured them all possible support. No one is to blame that this had not been done except Messrs Potts and Bull.'

At the opening of the Council meeting on the 13th of October the President, Mr Smith, read aloud a letter from Mr Watmough, Hemsworth delegate, as follows:

'Holly Bank, Hemsworth, Oct 8, 1906.

Dear Mr Wadsworth,.... I wish to explain to you the reason I will not be attending today's Council and you will no doubt be aware that at our last Council I made a statement to the effect that I would at any time stand to one side to allow Mr Potts or Bull to attend Council so as to be able to defend themselves. Now on Wednesday morning last, at our Committee he was asked to attend the Council, but for some reason or other he objected, and said it would be better for an independent man to go, which of course I objected to and said if he did not want to attend I should certainly attend myself. Now nothing more was said of this neither in our general meeting or anywhere else as I am aware of until Sunday Morning, I received a note from Mr Potts which states as follows: I have decided to attend Tuesday's Council meeting as delegate. You will receive the wages. Please confirm —J. Potts. So I have agreed to let him attend, so as to be able to defend his own case. But I don't want the Council to discuss anything in regards to myself, as I wish to be present when that takes place, as I can soon rectify and repeat what I said in the Council, for I still say that I was not aware of any one being authorised or deputed to attend the Liverpool Congress. Hoping this will do for me.

I remain yours sincerely
Thos. Watmough.'

After hearing Mr Watmough's letter, Potts volunteered to *'retire until it was settled'* and walked towards the door. Following comments from the chair Potts returned to his seat and was asked to state his case. Before managing to so do he was subjected to long blistering attacks from the Chairman, Mr Wadsworth, and Mr Hall. The attacks included accusations of:

'Criticising the Officials, criticising the Nominations for the Hallamshire election, calling for reductions of miners and M. P.'s pay, not being nominated to attend the T. U. C. congress, not collecting rent for the houses leased by the Miners Federation, as well as allegations that Hemsworth miners supporting Potts were

given between £10 and £12 from Nipsey Funds.'

In his attack John Wadsworth made an interesting statement with regard to the Y.M.A. not making an appeal for support at congress:

'The Hemsworth people, Potts and Bull, say: Why didn't the Officials appeal without being asked from Hemsworth? Well they didn't know we were not going to appeal; we would have appealed for the whole if we had appealed at all. There was something behind that, that a large and powerful organisation should have to apply to the Parliamentary Congress, because it has one, two or three collieries out on strike. Is it going to appeal for support and lower its dignity. This is a Society before all other Societies. It is a disgrace to this Society to ever make such appeals, because you have got two or three Collieries out, don't you think you will have appeals to assist them. In fact you will have scores and hundreds—hundreds in far worse position financially and numerically, than the Yorkshire Miners Association.... I hope we are not going to appeal as a society, if we cadge voluntarily that is another thing. They want to make it a compulsory affair and it is a shame.'

When Potts was eventually allowed to put his case to the delegates, he challenged the accuracy of the accusations and allegations made by the Y.M.A. officers, then chastised them for not allowing him time to prepare a detailed rebuttal of the statements. He then persuaded the meeting that the Y.M.A headquarters distribute leaflets outlining the accusations and his rebuttal of these, to all branches to let them decide the issue. These tactics enabled Potts to attract a majority of almost 10,000 against the motion asking for the *Dismemberment of Potts and Bull*. Having won the battle, Potts and Bull were free to continue their union activities.

In the same week the one-year lease of houses obtained by the £1,000 grant from the Miners Federation of Great Britain, expired.

The houses were returned to Mr Betts, the owner, and notices to quit by the 6th of November issued to the occupants.

The issue of the miners paying rent to the Miners Federation who had leased the houses from Mr Betts caused some major problems for the Hemsworth branch officials. In the beginning it was decided families who could afford to pay should pay 4 shillings per week, (substantially less than rent in the area which was between 5 shillings and 6 pence to 6 shillings and 3 pence per week), families who could not afford to pay did not need to pay. The outcome of this policy was divisive, some families paid little rent, many paid no rent, both of which caused resentment among the families in Hemsworth and Kinsley who were obliged to pay rent to their landlords from the same amount of income as the families living in Betts' houses. The miner's committee finally abandoned all attempts to collect the rent money in June when the total collected was £89-3s-0d, which left the federation with an additional bill for £1,200.

In September a letter was received by the Federation informing them two months rent was due (£177-4s-0d) plus one other item of £7-10s-0d. However the only money paid to the organisation was £38-16s-7d, as a result the Federation had decided to make another grant to pay the total amount incurred in leasing the premises from Mr Betts.

It is interesting to note the emergence of John Potts' son as speaker at the weekly I.L.P. discussions. With W. Bull presiding, young Potts delivered his paper then took questions from the floor on the question of *Is War Necessary?*

The I.L.P. continued to hold indoor meetings in the hut at Kinsley, in the Kinsley Hotel and in the union branch room in the Kings Head Hotel in Hemsworth.

During summer months however the I.L.P. and Christian groups held open air meetings at *Crosshill* in Hemsworth. The use of Crosshill as a venue for these meetings came under threat in the first week of October as the local Police raised objections to it being so used. Since the I.L.P. had finished its open air meetings for the year there was no immediate problem, nevertheless the local I.L.P. officials clearly expressed their intention of testing the police in springtime.

On the 9th of October as families received their *Nipsey Money* a bonus of a ¼lb tin of Messrs Rowntree and Fry was given to every member. Two days later an anonymous friend donated a barrel of fish and eight boxes of kippers for families. One week later *The Grimsby Fish Supply Company* of Barnsley Road in Hemsworth donated free fish dinners to almost every family in Hemsworth and Kinsley. Approximately two tons of fish were given away with the beleaguered staff having to deal with a queue of almost 600 people at the busiest time.

Following the Miners Federation Ballot on the question of whether the federation should join the Labour Representation Committee, Hall and Wadsworth addressed a meeting supporting the Liberal and Labour case at Stourton in Leeds. Again the view of John Wadsworth on the Labour Representation Committee was made clear:

'He was glad to say that the Miners Federation had decided by a majority of 10,000 not to join.' When questioned about the voting in Yorkshire: *'17,399 voted for affiliation, 12,730 voted against. Total membership of the Y.M.A. was 60,471, only 30,129 voted leaving 30,342 who did not vote.'* In his opinion they refrained from voting because *'they were satisfied with the present condition of things.'* Continuing this theme he advised them:

'Study the principles of Socialism and if you believe in Trade Unionism you can't be socialists. Socialists set out to defeat trade unionists and not only trade unionists but Co-operatives as well.'

As time dragged on the condition of the pit began to cause concern;

the owners had allegedly issued the statement that '*no old men were wanted*', which they claimed was only relevant in their request for men to clear the falls of debris in the underground roads and *gates* in readiness for re-commencement of work. The miners voiced their objections to the request:

'Does he expect we are going to allow young men to work down the pit to help in clearing it so that the owners can bring in Blacklegs or anybody they like after they have submitted to us such a wretched price list on Chinese Compound Terms.'

Since they were unable to recruit young, local men to work on the roof falls, Mr Shaw made it known that it would now be impossible to re-open the pit before the New Year.

Prior to the introduction of the *Welfare State* age was not the determinant of whether one could be employed, it was judged solely on the person's ability to '*do a full days work*'. An example of the life-work cycle of a male miner is included for information:

'John and Selina Wileman both 71 of Fitzwilliam Terrace celebrated their golden anniversary. Both were born in Mesham, Leicestershire in 1835. They had 10 children, 6 were still living and married. The four sons and two daughters had given them 24 grandchildren and 4 great-grandchildren. Mr Wileman intends working in the pit again when the strike ends'. He '*started in the pits aged 9 and had never lost a day's work through sickness up to the strike.*'

Evidence of a hardening of attitude of some of the trade union bodies towards the Hemsworth miners was seen at the Executive Committee Meeting of the International Federation of Trade and Labour Unions, who refused a request for assistance from the Hemsworth men on the grounds that the Executive could not see their way to grant strike benefits, the men never having worked for the new owner.

In a similar vein it was reported in early November that the Y.M.A:

'Told the men that unless they showed a better spirit and endeavoured to end the strike early, a ballot of the county would be taken on the matter.'

With only three days left before the families had to vacate the houses leased by the Miners Federation tension rose as the threat of eviction drew nearer and the prospect of going back to the tents loomed closer; in the final event their fears were unfounded:

'Mr Betts took on as tenants all those who lived in them under the Miners Federation. He has promised to pay back 1/- per week to all those who pay rent regularly.'

Collectors were still being despatched to the surrounding area to raise money for the *Nipsey Fund* which had been paying out approximately 2 shillings and 6 pence per week. The young Gabriel Price, now in charge of the *Nipsey Fund*, reported a discrepancy of £11-1s-11d between the money given to one collector (£36-19s-2½d), and the amount received by the *Nipsey Fund*. When challenged the collector admitted his guilt and was subsequently charged with *Misappropriation*. The decision was taken with some reluctance, however the relief committee justified its decision on two grounds: firstly the belief that miner's funds should be protected, and secondly to show contributors their donations were properly handled. At the accused man's trial a spokesman for the committee asked for leniency because the man had been a collector for some time and this was his first offence. The magistrate sentenced the man to one month in prison.

A further degree of complexity was added to the dispute when Major Shaw informed the local miner's branch:

'He will hold no further negotiations with men who are not directly affected by the dispute.'

This meant that workers previously employed in the Shafton Seam which would not be re-opened would be excluded from talks on the future of the colliery.

Immediately after this announcement the local Y.M.A. branch passed a resolution excluding Shafton men from taking part in any further negotiations. The implications of this decision caused mixed feelings in the Township. One camp believed Potts, who had been a Checkweighman at Shafton, would still be included in his role as Branch Secretary. The other camp rejoiced because they believed this meant the exclusion of Potts. The split in the Hemsworth branch was reflected in South Kirkby Y.M.A branch where some ugly scenes were recorded at a meeting of the Hemsworth men working at South Kirkby, and members of that Y.M.A. branch. An eye witness account of the proceedings describes these tensions as follows:

'*The meeting had just been started when Mr Walsh rose and asked the chairman why the meeting had not been called for the previous evening, according to promise. A reply was given this was owing to a misunderstanding between the Secretary and the sub-checkweighman in the Barnsley seam. This explanation did not appear to satisfy the questioner, but the matter was dropped. The meeting went quietly on for about quarter of an hour, when someone put in a query as to the Butty System. Mr Walsh rose to address the meeting but chair called him to order as there was another speaker on his feet. Mr Walsh declined to give way, this led to a heated altercation between him and the chairman in the course of which the disturber called Mr Exley a Liar. Mr Exley called him ditto and in time each inserted a few expletives which were more forcible than polite.*

Eventually Mr Walsh (who had been gradually drawing nearer to the chairman's seat), gave Mr Exley a push and called him a Fryston Blackleg whereupon Mr Exley retaliated with a Dab on the

Ear, which knocked Mr Walsh backwards. Mr Walsh's friends tried to pull him away and several men rushed to protect their president and stood in a fighting attitude round him. The meeting was closed, leaving business unfinished.'

The politicisation of Hemsworth and Kinsley manifested itself in other ways: During the week ending the 24th of November two hundred and fifty Roman Catholics went by special train to Leeds to take part in a demonstration against the Education Bill. The Hemsworth contingent carried a large green banner proclaiming:

'*Hemsworth Will Never Surrender Our Schools.'*

The main issue for the Hemsworth contingent was the plight of Mrs Hollis, a school cleaner whose contract had finished on the 3rd of November 1906. Prior to the schools being taken over by the county council the managers paid her £1-0s-0d per week. This was reduced to 12 shillings and 6 pence per week then further reduced to 8 shillings per week, out of which she had to buy materials for cleaning.

The Hemsworth Education sub-committee refused to appoint anyone at this wage. As a consequence teachers had to wait until 9.15am before they could get into school, light the fires and generally prepare the classrooms. The following Monday parents started keeping their children off school in protest. A Mrs Simpson was then given the job without consultation with the Hemsworth Education Sub-Committee and against the wishes of the school; thus the motivation for the Hemsworth contingent.

It would appear that the Shaw family resented trade unions interfering in any of their collieries, not only in Hemsworth:

'*Tom Exley, President of nearby South Kirkby Y.M.A. branch received 14 days Notice to leave the pit. Mr Exley was the seventh committee member to be discharged during his tenure of office.*

More importantly, he was the second President out of the last three to be sacked. Feelings ran high over this issue, many miners advocating a strike in support of their President, with the issue to be referred to the Y. M.A. officials for advice.'

A mass meeting of the Hemsworth branch was held during the week ending the 15th of December 1906 to discuss the Conciliation Board's proposal. The offer gave the men a 5% wage rise beginning in January which would be reviewed after two years. This offer was unanimously rejected by the miners; later during the same meeting the branch gave its support to Johnny Guest of South Heindley in the election of the Vice President of the Y.M.A.

In week 122 of the strike the *Nipsey Fund* records showed donations of £50 from the Lanarkshire miners plus another £50 from Barrow Hematite. This enabled £106-4s-6d *Nipsey Money* to be paid out that week (December the 11th). To help families with Christmas expenses this was increased to £130-0s-6d.

At the branch's half yearly meeting held the following day the following members were elected:

***'President:-** J Benson.*
***Secretary:-** John Potts.*
***Treasurer:-** E. Ferriday.*
***Delegate to Y. M.A:-** A. Goddard.*
***Committee Members**:- W. O .Bull (Shafton), T. Stollard and T. Ainley (Barnsley Bed), E. Smith and J. Glover (Haigh Moor)'.*

Although the Shafton Seam was never likely to be re-opened the men from that seam retained their representation in their union branch.

Once again Tom Elstone of the Kinsley Hotel began to raise funds for the miner's children. This time however his intention was to provide the children with a treat during the festive period; as the townspeople became aware of Tom's intentions they raised a further £32 bringing his total to £60 which ensured:

'Every striker's child from Hemsworth, Kinsley, Ackworth, and Featherstone, received a good meal with entertainment, as well as getting a gift of sweets and either a scarf, a wrap, stockings or a Tam O'Shanter, plus a bag containing an apple, an orange, and bun or cake.'

On New Years Eve Mr Elstone again initiated a treat for the Children of the Township:

'At 4 o'clock 600 children met in the market place then adjourned to the Primitive Methodist Mission Hall.... During 4 sittings the children were treated to a splendid Ham Tea with cakes and buns... all got an apple and orange plus a scarf or shawl on their way home.... The 30 orphans had a special present donated by C. Turner from Hemsworth Post Office.'

The generosity of the mining community was in evidence again: J. C. Green, the local baker, donated his baking, this was augmented by donations from E. Burns of the Victoria Hotel, T. Tait of the Kings Head, and J. Sparling of Burnley. Cudworth I.L.P. branch despatched a Father Christmas who arrived at the party with a cart laden with gifts of small articles of woollen clothing, 2 fowls (to be sold at Hemsworth market) 19 dozen oranges, apples, sweets and 25 shillings in cash. The proceedings were organised by H. Goddard, G. Price, G. Ainley, J. Hanson, W. E Smith and J. Goddard, with Mr Elstone again acknowledged as the initiator.

The *Nipsey Fund* of week 124 in its itemised accounts carried an unusual entry for the 26th of December:

'£29-14s-0d paid to victims to make them equal with men locked out and on strike.'

Nothing else is recorded to help us identify who exactly these were.

January 1907 arrived in a township whose future was shrouded in a blend of hope and despair; a number of colliers had abandoned hope of the pit re-opening and found employment elsewhere:

'Between 60 and 70 men were walking every day to Grimethorpe Colliery, a journey of approximately 4 miles each way.'

The more optimistic believed the pit would be re-started with them being employed by the new owners. Whilst the miners waited on an end to their dispute, the council continued to develop public housing in the area with the opening of the new stone built houses in the West End of Hemsworth, this was augmented by the opening of a New School costing £5,467; designed to provide capacity for 600 children it was:

'acknowledged to be the finest of its kind in the Country.'

For members of the Potts family the New Year brought deep personal tragedy with the death of Mrs Potts. Among the many letters of condolence was one from the local *Women's Social and Political Union* in recognition of Mrs Potts personal contribution to their cause. Indeed Mrs Potts and the Women's Social and Political Union had been at the very heart of the growing political awareness and activities of the women of Hemsworth and Kinsley. For example, on January the 14th:

'Believers and non-believers in votes for women flocked in large numbers to Kinsley—to hear the adventures of one of the most famous batch of women who recently suffered in Holloway gaol for the cause they had at heart, and which cause they hoped to force in the House of Commons.'

Mrs Goddard presided over the meeting held in the Kinsley Hotel, in her opening address:

'She expressed hope that those present who had not yet joined the Women's Social and Political Union would do so when they heard what the speaker had to say.'

Miss Gawthorpe, a school teacher from Leeds:

'Spoke for over 2 hours with frequent applause testifying to the interest taken in her speech. She spoke about the experience in Holloway, the fight she had waged against Sam Evans the M. P. for Mid Glamorgan, and claimed the Miners Executive, The Miners House of Lords, were afraid to bring out a candidate against him and therefore let him continue as an M. P. as well as being recently made the Recorder for Swansea.'

The passion from Miss Gawthorp's talk generated much enthusiasm among the women in the village resulting in a large attendance at a subsequent meeting in Kinsley on the 23rd of January, where many women found their voice on the topic of *'Should Women Have the Right to Vote in Parliamentary Elections.'* The women of the Township were so enthused that it was arranged for a delegation of six from their ranks to attend a Suffragette Lobby of Parliament planned for Wednesday the 13th of February; the funds to cover their expenses being advanced by a London based group. It is not recorded if any of the local women took part in this Lobby of Parliament, however 800 women did attend, with a total of 60 arrests being made.

Immediately before the delegates were due to leave for the Suffragette demonstration the limitations and problems of long distance communications became apparent, playing havoc with the plans of one delegate. According to the Wakefield Express:

'Mrs Barnsley, one of the most enthusiastic women in the neighbourhood in matters of Social Reform was to be in the party. On Monday, the day before she set off, Mrs Barnsley received a

telegram message telling her Joe was dead. Her trip to London was therefore cancelled.'

As the story unfolded, her husband, Joe, had set off on Saturday morning intending to walk part of the way to the city of Durham where he would visit members of his family. On Monday morning a telegram from Joe's sister in Durham informed Mrs Barnsley *'Joe arrived dead.'*

The stricken woman, along with her brother in law Noah, left for Durham on Monday afternoon. As the news leaked out villager's blinds were drawn.

The morning after another relative received a telegram: *'JOE ALIVE AND WELL'*. A letter followed. It appears that the first message should have read: *'Joe arrived dead tired'*, though whether the omission of the last word was the fault of the sender or the Post Office no one knows.

The increasing politicisation and open hostility of the women towards miners now working the pit appeared to cause concern to the male unionists who passed the following resolution:

'That the women should leave these men, who were working, alone, and let them deal with them; and that the people should not trade with the trades people of the district who were supplying these men, now working at the colliery, with provisions.'

It seems the men themselves were trying to identify who was working at the Hemsworth pit in order to put pressure on them to stop doing so.

The Hemsworth men working at South Kirkby tried again to elect officers for their Y. M. A. branch. Unfortunately this meeting suffered the same fate as the previous one, being abandoned before any business was done. Nothing of significance was reported on the meeting held during the following weeks.

As the exodus of families continued, it was reported:

'Six families were preparing for emigration to New Zealand'.

The Shaw's displayed their intention of being in the township for the long haul by releasing the news they were *'considering erecting 77 houses near the pit.'*

Of the existing miner's cottages, now shrouded in decay and depression, the same correspondent wrote:

'Kinsley is almost like Goldsmith's Deserted Village, everything about the place looks lost.'

In a display of solidarity with their *Trade Union brothers in Yorkshire,* G. Warner, Secretary of Walworth Coal Porters Union, addressed the local I.L.P gathering, asking them to make arrangements for his Union's annual June Feast to be held in Hemsworth and Kinsley.

On Saturday the 9th of February in Kinsley itself, the local I.L.P. societies met to select candidates to stand in the Local Elections. John Guest was selected as candidate for the County Council Election with Ike Burns and A. Goddard selected for the Rural Council Election.

On Wednesday the 23rd of February several hundred loaves were distributed to needy cases. The bread was provided from surplus funds left over after paying all the expenses of the children's treat which had been given to commemorate the opening of West End School. The following week the Coronation Club gave 3 shillings to every woman and 1 shilling and 6 pence for every child to families in Kinsley.

Whilst nothing appeared to be happening in talks between the Y.M.A. and the Shaw family, a growing antagonism towards the miner's union was highlighted by Fred Hall of the Y.M.A. in referring to a letter displaying the strong anti-union feeling emanating from the Coal Owners. By the beginning of March almost 200 men and boys from Hemsworth and Kinsley were working at Grimethorpe Colliery, which though welcome, was not without problems. As was the custom of the time doctor's fees were deducted from the men's wages each fortnight, however the distance between Grimethorpe and Hemsworth and Kinsley meant it was impossible to get the pit doctor to attend all cases of sickness in the area. The men subsequently complained about this and suggested a list of Hemsworth based miners be compiled and their doctor's fees paid to a local doctor. By the middle of the month approximately 1000 men and boys from the township had found work in other pits; in addition to the men working at Grimethorpe a large number were working at South Kirkby, Nostell, Featherstone, Monkton and Old Carlton Collieries. As one reporter commented:

'It would seem as if they were being gradually starved into getting work, only dire distress will cause a man to walk 6/7 or even 8 miles a day to his work and 8 miles back.'

The building of a model village near the pit which had been proposed by the colliery owners a few months earlier was now opposed by local tradesmen who were suffering from the lack of spending power in the Township.

The I.L.P. re-commenced its open air meetings at Crosshills with John Potts giving a talk on Local Politics. As they had promised, the local police stopped the meeting and arrested Potts and Bull who were subsequently summoned to appear before the magistrates at Pontefract.

On the political front; the Labour candidates for the Hemsworth Councillors and Guardians consisted of: Ike Burns. G. Price, W. O. Bull, A. Goddard and E. Fereday. When the results were announced only Gabriel Price and John Potts, who had opted to contest a seat in Ackworth, were defeated. The strength of the Hemsworth Labour group was added to by the success of A. Jagger (Shafton) and T. Elliot (South Heindley), these six were in effect the first Labour Group on the Town Council.

Further evidence of the waning of support from fellow Unionists can be seen in the 7th Annual report of the National and International Federation of Trade and Labour Unions. The Secretary referring to the Hemsworth dispute said:

'The commencement in 1906 found us expecting an early settlement of the Hemsworth dispute, but the unexpected happened by the Company going into liquidation. As the men had no dispute with the liquidator we ceased to pay strike benefit. A friend Company eventually bought the Collieries. They failed to induce the men to start work at the prices offered. We held, that as the men had never worked for the new Company, they could not be regarded as entitled to strike benefit, but, were simply in the same situation as unemployed workmen, who would not start work where it was offered them because the wage offered was not upto the standard. Whatever dissatisfaction there may be among these members owing to the stoppage of their strike benefits the fact remains that we as a Federation have loyally supported them while they had a clear case of being in dispute.

We have paid in all the sum of £2,455-2s-10d in support of the dispute, much of the sum, £1,871-2s-9d was paid previous to 1906. This represents an average of £1-15s-6d per member which has been paid in levies in support of the dispute. The continued call for levies in support of the above has resulted in 296 members having lapsed during this year. Out of this number I find that no less than 243 are miners.'

By the 6th of April 1907 more than two and half years since the beginning of the dispute, the miners continued to lobby support for their cause; to this end a deputation was sent to Cardiff to lobby the South Wales Miners Federation who donated a further £50, and in return they instructed Mr Abraham M. P. to ascertain precisely what had been done to find a solution to the dispute.

It was noted the following week, on the 13th of April, the South Kirkby, Featherston and Hemsworth Colliery Company filed particulars of the £20,000, 4½% debentures created by resolution last August and September, which were secured by a trust deed.

The trust group had been registered as: J. Shaw of Kirkbymoorside and J. R. Shaw of Purston Hall.

The *Nipsey Fund* for week 139, Tuesday the 9th of April, registering money received and paid out on, refers once again to victims in its entries: '*7 victims 2 shillings each. 14s-0d.*'

It is interesting to note that *Nipsey Money* for week 141 paid out on the 23rd of April was 2 shillings. However a levy of 6 pence per man was imposed to help meet the costs of Potts and Bull when they attended Pontefract Court to answer summons issued as a result of the I.L P meeting in Crosshills which had been halted by the police. Little or nothing was reported on the Hemsworth dispute during the next few weeks, however it was reported:

'The West Yorkshire Coal Owners on Tuesday arranged to at once increase the price of all classes of engine coal 6d per ton as the men will also receive a 5% increase in their wages.'

In the township a new arena of conflict between employer and employees was brought to the public's attention:

'On Sunday morning prior to matins at the Parish church a number of choir boys interviewed the Rector (R.H.Gilbert) with matters they

allege to be grievances. The rector told them, it would be impossible for him to give them a supper this time, but he would see that they went with the choir men next time, he would give them 6d extra next choir trip.'

In this instance negotiations were successful in averting a prolonged dispute.

By early May 1907 it was known that several men, not including deputies, were working at the colliery; the anger caused by this news was exacerbated as miners became aware an increasing number of *Blacklegs* were being brought in to work the collieries. As a consequence police had to escort the *Blacklegs* home from the 2 o'clock and 6 o'clock shifts as the crowds of miners tried to vent their anger on them.

On Wednesday evening of the 8th of May a large crowd gathered near the gas works to wait for the Deputies and *Blacklegs* coming home:

'Police constables lined up across the road to keep the crowd back as mounted police escorted the Blacklegs up the hill to Hemsworth where they lived. The men had got nearly up Shay Hill when the crowd broke through. Mounted men seeing the plight of their colleagues charged the crowd driving them back into the village streets. One man was knocked down; his mate grabbed the horse's bridle and brought the horse to a stop. The crowd dispersed but met again to hold a large demonstration. Hundreds of flags and many banners were carried by the crowd, which included youths and children. The Banners included ***Hemsworth Lock out Miners Children*** *and* ***Hemsworth Miners Children Defend Umpires Award****. To the accompaniment of an indescribable din produced by beating tin cans, pots and pans and the playing of mouth organs, accordions, tin whistles and trumpets they set off round*

the village carrying effigies of blacklegs (very well made and detailed). They also carried a woollen sheep blackened to make it represent a ***Blacksheep*** *carried on a long pole. They then made their way to Hemsworth, when near the Church saw a deputy. The crowd rushed for him, caught him and pelted him with dirt sods and* ***Opprobrious Epithets,*** *then drove him all the way home.'*

From that day on constables escorted the *Blacklegs* whilst Superintendent Hollis kept a close eye on events by driving around the village in his pony and trap.

On the 24th of May 1907 at the Y.M.A. branch meeting in the Kings Head Hotel, it was decided *'to re-open negotiations with Major Shaw'* with a view to ending the dispute. Inherent in this decision was the agreement:

'To return to work on a reduction of 1½d per ton on the Barnsley Seam, 4d per ton ***End On*** *work, and 2d per ton* ***Bord On*** *for the Haigh Moor Seam.'*

This was well short of Major Shaw's last offer of a reduction of 5 pence for all types of work.

Major Shaw's response to the miner's offer was contained in a letter to the Y.M.A. and a special meeting was quickly organised to discuss this. Major Shaw's letter left the assembly in no doubt:

'The offer he had made was the final one and he therefore could not entertain a further meeting.' It went on to explain that Major Shaw: *'Was working the colliery at a much greater cost than the other Collieries and as the prices were higher than at these other pits, if the men accepted his terms they would be getting a bigger share of the profits.'*

After hearing Major Shaw's response the miners agreed to stick to the terms they had offered him. Many of them believed the struggle was only just beginning, though equally, many of their ranks hoped Major Shaw's statement would bring about the collapse of the strike.

Unmindful of the previous request from their husbands, the miner's wives continued to vent their feelings on the *Blacklegs* working the colliery. As a consequence of their actions Catherine Glynn, Elizabeth Taite, Mark Walter, Elizabeth Roper, Martha Pugh, Rose Smith and Malvina Richards appeared at Pontefract West Riding Court. The charges levied at the instigation of the Colliery Company, included *Persistently Following, Following in a Disorderly Manner* and *Intimidation,* all of which were brought under the Conspiracy Act. After much bargaining the defendants were *Bound Over* for six months and ordered to pay costs.

Spirits in the Township were lifted the following week when the Y.M.A. gave all the Kinsley miners a free rail ticket plus 1 shilling spending money to enable them to attend the Y.M.A.'s Annual Demonstration in Barnsley.

Major Shaw's long term view of the Hemsworth Colliery was beginning to emerge as work commenced on building homes for his colliers in a *New Village* located between the pit and the coke ovens.

On the 18th of June in a display of solidarity with their trade union colleagues, 50 members of the Coal Porters Union left London at 11.30.pm on route to Hemsworth. On their arrival at 7.30 the following morning they were welcomed by the Kinsley brass band plus a large group of colliers proudly carrying their banners. The parade of Coal Porters and Coal Diggers, led by the band, marched up the hill from the station towards Hemsworth and breakfast at the Kings Head Hotel.

After breakfast the parade toured Kinsley where a free Gala had been laid on for the miners and their guests. Following the Gala the Coal

Porters were treated to one concert in the Kinsley Hotel and a second in the Kings Head before boarding the train at 11.30 p.m. to begin their journey home.

Tom Watmough, who had been replaced as the branch's delegate to the Y.M.A Council after the failed *dismemberment case,* continued his union work being appointed in June as General Secretary of the National and International Federation of Trade and Labour Unions, a position he held for approximately two months before he resigned.

The six monthly election of branch officers resulted in some new committee men being elected, these included:

'***President:*** *J. Benson.*
Treasurer: *Enoch Fereday.*
Secretary: *J. Potts.*
Committee members: *W. O. Bull, W. E. Smith, T. Batten, M. Tate and T. Stollard.*
Bellman: *Peter Kelly.*
Checkweigh Fund Secretary: *G.Stones.*
Treasurer: *W. Mills.'*

The ill-feeling between the South Kirkby and Hemsworth Y. M. A. branches continued to fester, with the South Kirkby branch refusing to raise the 6 pence levy on members imposed by the Y.M.A. to help the Hemsworth miner's families.

Nipsey Accounts for Tuesday June the 25th give details of expenditure of the fund including money paid out for the Coal Porters gala:

'Total income	*£146 - 3s - 0d*
Kinsley Prize Band	*£4 - 0s - 0d*
Expenses of collectors	*£54 - 3s - 8½d*
Paid men for work done (travel etc)	*£6 - 17s - 6d*
Balance sheets, stationery, circulars:	*£4 - 19s - 8d*

Accident Society for Doctor	*£5 - 0s - 0d*
Amount carried forward	*£9 - 5s - 8½d'*

Accounts for the *Nipsey Fund* for the 150th week of the strike published in the local newspaper of the 6th of July show:

'Income by Grants.	*£167 - 7s - 3d*
Income from collecting books	*£60 - 15s - 2½d*
Brought forward	*£2 - 7s - 1½d*
Amount for distribution	*£230 - 9s - 7d'*

On Saturday the 28th of July Major Shaw and John Potts, Hemsworth Y.M.A. secretary, faced each other across the courtroom of Pontefract magistrates court as Samuel Bell, a striking miner, was charged under The Conspiracy Act of 1875 with intimidation and using threats against Isaac Chadburn. Chadburn had moved from Rotherham to Kinsley pit to work as a contractor two weeks before the alleged incident.

In his opening address Mr Clayton-Smith representing Chadburn addressed the bench:

'The offence was a serious one, as the chairman, an employer of labour, would know full well, and also if this offence was not nipped in the bud how very serious the consequences might be.'

In his evidence Chadburn claimed he was walking near his home on the 22nd of July when Bell approached him:

'Pulled a pocket knife from one of his right hand pockets... said I will cut your... heart out if you go to work at Kinsley colliery again.'

Chadburn's story was supported by testimony from Samuel Hyde, a pit deputy, who claimed he saw the defendant pull the knife from his pocket and say:

'Come on you... nigger, will rip your... heart out if... you go to work at the colliery again.'

John Wheatley, another miner working at the pit, corroborated Hyde's version of events. In his opening, Clem Edwards K.C, M.P for Chester, representing the defendant, argued the prosecutor had not proved his case. Indeed he had even called the policemen who attended the incident as objective witnesses. In view of these shortcomings his client had no charges to answer. Before closing he called three witnesses: George Stone, J. Westwood and Mary Wagstaffe who gave evidence supporting the accused claim that he did not have a knife. Having listened to both sides the chairman informed the accused:

'They were perfectly satisfied that there had been intimidation and that the defendant had produced a knife.'

Sam Bell received a £3 fine plus £1-11s-6d costs or one months imprisonment.

The tranquillity of the township was shattered during the fourth week of July with the arrival of another 12 new miners, provoking another outbreak of anger with some:

'230 people waiting to boo and insult the Blacklegs.'

In spite of local collier's actions, Major Shaw showed his commitment to his colliery in two distinct ways: Firstly the houses in the *Model Village* at Kinsley were almost completed, needing only a final coat of plaster to finish them, secondly he was filling an increasing number of houses in New Row and Outgang Terrace with *Incomers* to work at his colliery.

As well as the pressure being applied by the colliery owners, the Hemsworth men began to experience increasing resistance from the ranks of their own union. The Y.M.A Council meeting in early August 1907 voted 2 to 1 in favour of raising a levy on members to help the Hemsworth miners, however the President, Herbert Smith, ruled that this could not be implemented. Mr Smith's action caused a great deal of consternation among the Hemsworth men who made a number of protests to him. Three weeks later the Y.M.A decided to ballot its members on the question of paying a compulsory levy of 3 pence (for full members) and 1½ pence (for half members). The result of this ballot announced in early October showed a majority of 2000 in favour of the levy, however under Y.M.A. rules it required a two thirds majority to implement such action, the levy could not therefore be imposed.

Open hostility towards the *Blacklegs* continued to manifest itself. On Monday the 26th of August:

'Between 9 and 10 o'clock a large crowd gathered in the village waiting for the afternoon shift to come home. The police tried to move one man on—he refused—some say he was then arrested. The crowd then rushed the police and set the man free—Bottles, Jugs and chip pans being thrown at the police.'

The demonstration continued on Tuesday night with large crowds assembling once again in the village:

'They heard the tramp, tramp as 12 Blacklegs surrounded by police, four walking, four on horseback, two horses at the front, two horses at the back. As they approached the village, coming down Shay Hill they were met by a volley of stones and missiles. The mounted police charged driving people into two side streets; the rest of the police hurried the Blacklegs through. Before the mounted police had fully returned to the escort, they were attracted back by some of their colleagues calling them back to the village. All the police rushed back leaving the Blacklegs to walk alone. The police saved their colleagues. The men dispersed but formed back up into gangs… again they were charged by the police… this continued until well after midnight.'

As a result of this night's demonstration:

'One burly sergeant had the side of his face badly cut, and a piece of his ear taken off. Several other constables were badly hurt. A number of the Blacklegs were also hurt, one was hit in 3 places and another had to be taken to Hemsworth to have 3 stitches put in a hand wound.'

In response to appeals from local miner's leaders to end the violence towards the *Blacklegs,* aided no doubt by a massive police presence, peace returned to the township on Wednesday night.

In mid September the Y.M.A appealed to the Trade Union Congress for assistance for the miners on strike or locked-out at Hemsworth, Frickley and Thrybergh Hall Collieries. In setting out their case the Y.M.A. informed the T .U. C. the Hemsworth miners had been out nearly 3 years, Frickley miners had been out 20 weeks and miners at Thrybergh Hall for nearly 3 years. It is interesting to note that Thrybergh Hall miners had been on strike for the same length of time as the Hemsworth colliers. John Potts had written to their secretary asking them to wage a joint campaign; however this was not replied to. From the documents available it would seem Thrybergh miners were less effective than their Hemsworth colleagues in publicising their case.

During the time these collieries were on strike, Y.M.A members at these collieries received 9 shillings per week strike and lock out pay plus 1 shilling per week for each child under 13 years of age.

The Association had already paid out: *'To Hemsworth £84,000, to Thrybergh Hall £50,000 and to Frickley £600. During the past six years the Association has spent £365,000 in strikes and lock outs. The present appeal is made to help the men, women and children to a get a little more food than their rule allowance allows.'*

The following week (ending the 23rd of September), Messrs Bradley, Backhouse and Taylor appeared at Pontefract West Riding Court to answer charges of *Obstructing the Footpath* and *Assault on the Police*. James Batton appeared at the same session charged with *Using Violent Language*. They were all found guilty and formally *Bound Over* to keep the peace for 6 months.

Improvements in the township continued with the new Rural Council borrowing and spending £1,135 for improvements to the sewer system to enable 200 new houses to be linked to the sewage network. Though the anticipation of the ending of the strike was marred by the fear that when the miners began to earn wages again their families would shop in Wakefield and Barnsley markets in search of bargains and produce; to the casual passer-by Kinsley appeared prosperous with little to remind one of:

'The memorable scenes which have been witnessed in this little village, it is only when one gets into the bye-streets that the effects of the evictions and riots are seen.'

Throughout this time Fred Hall and other Y.M.A. leaders had been working strenuously for a settlement of the strike at Hemsworth. A meeting between Major Shaw, the Y.M.A and its local delegates was scheduled for early September, with Potts and Goddard elected to represent the local branch. Nothing was heard about the outcome of this until Wednesday the 8th of November when notices were posted at the miner's headquarters informing them officials from Barnsley would address the men on what had taken place at their branch meeting on Wednesday morning.

Later that morning a fragment of the once mighty army of over 1000 miners gathered as Y.M.A. officers Fred Hall M.P., Herbert Smith and J. Wadsworth attended the meeting. Although it was held in private the local paper reported that Major Shaw had stated:

'Subject to his employing men from other collieries owned by him in the district for preparing the pits for work and doing other important work at present required......he will find employment in three months time for all men who remain in the district.'

It was however stressed that this was not official and should not be taken as being *'the terms of the settlement'*.

The following day as the men received their strike pay they recorded their votes on whether or not they should return to work. At a press conference on the 10th of November following the Y.M.A Executive meeting, the assembled group were informed that as a result of the ballot of Hemsworth miners:

'The terms which Major Shaw had offered had.....been officially accepted and the strike or lock out -whichever it may be called- was absolutely at an end. The executive has therefore instructed the committee to make all the necessary arrangements to get back to work as soon as possible.'

Two weeks later a notice was posted outside the branch headquarters at the Kings Head Hotel:

'The late workmen of the Hemsworth Colliery are hereby notified to attend the Colliery Office and sign the contract book in accordance with arrangements made by the Colliery Company and the general officials of the Yorkshire Miners Association.

John Potts, Branch secretary, Nov 26th 1907'

Some 300 miners made their way to the colliery to sign on for work. On Tuesday afternoon as around half-a-dozen of these men reported for work:

'There was quite a jubilant demonstration in Kinsley as ***Owd Ben Garbett****—along with—J Pye passed through the village to the*

pit—The sight of old Mr Garbett once more in the attire of a miner seems to have inspired them with hope that they too will be able to secure employment of some kind.'

Optimism about the quick end to the strike was encouraged by speeches given to the electorate of Hemsworth and Kinsley. Joe Walton, M.P for Barnsley, stressed the fact that since the removal of the 1 shilling per ton Coal Tax there had been an increase of 6,000,000 tons of coal exported in the first nine months of the year compared with the same period in 1906. He felt this must be good news for the Shafton Seam whose coal went for export. In addition with the abolition of the coal tax the colliery's costs would fall by £12,000 a year therefore the whole of the colliery should be more profitable.

Within the township the general feeling was one of intense relief tinged with guarded optimism about the future and sorrow that the terms of the settlement were less than generous. These sentiments were eloquently expressed by one local clergyman in a letter to the local newspaper which read:

'The men deserved the highest praise for the way they had conducted themselves during the dispute, especially when feeling was at such a tension as it had been on several occasions. He was sorry they had not received better terms of settlement after such a fine struggle.'

The newspaper continued its religious link in an article commemorating the consecration of the newly built church in Kinsley:

'By a remarkable coincidence the new Church of the Ascension at Kinsley was consecrated to the service of God on exactly the same day as the new price-list for the colliery was accepted. It is also remarkable that building operations were begun just about the time when the dispute first began, it is really looking as if a Devine hand had been at work in bringing the two things to a climax.'

As the majority of miners waited to re-start work at the pit, resentment grew at the continuing absence of officials from the Y.M.A. and the lack of detail on the terms of the settlement they had agreed with Major Shaw. A number of branch meetings had been held and resolutions passed, however these were never made public. It is highly likely these resolutions contained criticisms of both the Y. M. A. and the miners who had started work at the colliery. In a most unusual step the colliers who had resumed work issued a circular criticising Potts and the local branch:

'*We are charged with being tools of the Colliery Company, yet Mr Potts and his committee, in their circular, say it was agreed by the Yorkshire Miners Association Officials and (Mr Shaw of) the Colliery Company at the time of settlement, that men should be drafted from South Kirkby and Featherstone. We therefore wish to call your attention to the fact that our resuming work at Hemsworth is strictly in accordance with the settlement. Furthermore we wish to remind you that when the Yorkshire Miners Association Officials nearly two years ago were striving to obtain a settlement to the Hemsworth dispute, Mr Potts and his colleagues opposed them tooth and nail. On the other hand we did all in our power to back the officials and persuade the men to make a settlement. How our efforts were rewarded you well know, Potts and his party tried to hound us out of the locality. The statement that we gave an undertaking to resume work at Hemsworth in order to help the company to defeat the men is a deliberate lie. In conclusion, the present situation is the creation of Mr Potts and his tools, and they ought to be perfectly satisfied with it. We are appealing to the next council for permission to form a new branch of the Yorkshire Miners Association at Hemsworth, and we earnestly ask the support of the county to grant this request, as it is quite apparent Mr Potts and his party do not intend to give us fair play. Concannon, Watmough and Garbett will attend the offices on the date of the next council meeting and will be prepared to explain anything further that may be needed.*

Signatories to this statement are: Daniel Concannon, Thomas Watmough, Joseph Garbett, Peter Dooley, William Monaghan, John Riley, William Lincoln, G. Lincoln, Arthur Lincoln and P. Fleming.'

The strike committee instructed Potts to respond with a letter to the same newspaper putting their version of the facts into the public domain:

'There appears in your issue of the 6th inst report of a pit-gate meeting, presumed to have been held by the present employed Hemsworth workmen to protest against the Hemsworth Branch Committee refusing to accept the clearances of Messrs Watmough and Garbutt, though couched in terms to convey the impression that many were involved, and that Mr Lincoln was instructed by resolution to apply to the General Secretary of the Yorkshire Miners Association for permission to form a new branch. The report further conveys to the miners of Yorkshire that the principal officials of the association had asked them to state their ground of application. The officials at Barnsley never wrote for any such thing. We are informed that the meeting never took place. It is correct that the meeting was called, and preparation made to hold it on colliery premises but when the nature of the business for which the men were called together was made known to them, the bulk of the men walked away, declining to be advised by the meeting promoters. The resolution is presumed to have been moved by Mr J Perry, one of the workmen employed prior to the settlement, he being one of the persons Mr Lincoln so vindictively denounced as blacklegs in the branch room. The resolution can have no foundation in fact, as Mr Perry does not pay with us, neither has he tendered any clearance in fact, we do not know that he pays anywhere, or ever did.'

Pott's letter turned to Lincoln and Concannon, two stalwarts in the early days of the dispute who opted out of the strike to take up day jobs at South Kirkby Colliery at a higher than normal wage rate. After a fairly short period of time in these jobs they obtained clearance to transfer to Hemsworth Colliery where they were active in trying to break the strike. Indeed Potts went on to argue that they recruited another fifty workers into the Hemsworth Colliery, thereby denying striking colliers the chance of employment and imposing financial burdens on the Y.M.A. In addressing his comments to Lincoln, Potts claimed:

'This man's love and sincerity for the Association's welfare is proven by the fact that he himself is continuously unfinancial.'

For these reasons the Hemsworth branch would call on the Y.M.A to expel these men under rule 41 of the Y.M.A rule book.

When the motion requesting the formation of a new union branch at Hemsworth Colliery was raised during the Y.M.A. council meeting in Barnsley, it was countered by members of the existing branch calling for the *'dismemberment of all miners who signed the circular.'* Discussion of these two items occupied almost all of the meeting's time, however since no decision could be reached the item was shelved indefinitely.

When the issues were raised again the branch's request for dismemberment of Lincoln and Concannon was dismissed and a diktat issued that the Hemsworth branch should accept as members those miners working at Hemsworth Colliery who wished to join and be represented by the Y.M.A. The Hemsworth branch voted against complying with this decision by refusing to collect union dues from the men working at the colliery. In response to this direct challenge to their authority, strike pay to more than 200 men and their families was stopped until the branch conformed to the Council's decision.

With no viable alternative method of sustaining themselves and their families the branch conceded to the Y.M.A.

The following week as the men went to the lodge room in the Kings Head they were summoned to a meeting with three officials from Barnsley, although the meeting was private it was apparent that the branch had little option but to accept the decision of its governing body. This action further increased antagonism between the Y.M.A. officers and the local branch members, as one local journalist reported:

'There is much resentment expressed at the action of the Barnsley officials whom they consider overbearing and too officious. The new developments have also caused not a little uneasiness amongst the strikers as to their prospects for the coming winter.'

John Potts remained as branch secretary until the end of 1909 when, *'he kindly saw his way'* to retiring from this position thereby allowing working colliers to control the key positions in the branch. He did however continue to play a key role in local politics and in the Yorkshire Miners Union, in which he had strong grass roots support. In 1909 he was honoured by being selected by miners to speak on the same platform as Kier Hardie at the Yorkshire Miners annual gala. Ever true to his beliefs he continued to propound his case for the I. L. P. and its version of socialism.

To all intents and purposes the dispute was over, however many of the original colliers who went on strike were not reemployed and continued living on union strike pay until the middle of 1910 when the Yorkshire Miners Association declared the strike was officially ended.

From its troubled beginnings Hemsworth Colliery and indeed the township, which by this time included the new housing estate at Fitzwilliam as well as Kinsley, thrived for many years, until the decline of *Old Man Coal* and the round of pit closures in the latter part of the twentieth century.

However, that is another interesting story?

Note:
Howden of Denaby was the instigator of the legal action against the Y.M.A in the Cadeby and Denaby Main case being pursued through the courts.

CONCLUSION

At one level it may be argued that history should be seen as a collection of people, a series of events or incidents, which took place a long time ago and are irrelevant in today's sophisticated, highly technical age. Whilst this viewpoint may contain some truth, it would be rather foolish to believe there is nothing we can learn from the past. To paraphrase the words of one philosopher, those who do not learn from the mistakes of the past are bound to repeat them.

I believe society has learned that importing large numbers of workers and housing them in purpose built towns and villages in remote areas where the main source of employment is in a single industry such as coal mining, is not the best long-term option for the residents.

One has only to look at the problems blighting many of the former mining communities to see the effects the demise of the industry has had on the younger generations brought up in these conurbations, where there is little opportunity of the majority of them gaining useful employment; unless of course they are willing and able to commute to the nearest cities.

On a personal level, the main lesson I have learned from the Hemsworth story is the enormous power and ingenuity that can be harnessed when individuals unite to oppose an action or proposal they perceive to be morally unjust. This willingness of ordinary men and women to fight injustice for such a long period when their own living conditions were appalling and the odds so heavily stacked against them; is in itself remarkable.

However it must be understood that Hemsworth was by no means unique, its history of industrial relations has much in common with a large number of colliery towns in the British coalfield. In almost every part of the United Kingdom miners and their families were regularly evicted from their homes during strikes and lockouts. Hemsworth's uniqueness appears to rest on the manner in which the miners organised themselves to gain support from every corner of the U.K., and the manner in which they defended their local leaders in the face of strong criticism and personal attacks from the officials of the Y.M.A.

Whilst the Independent Labour Party was the dominant external political influence, the religious and moral convictions of the many Catholic and Methodist activists in the township gave an added strength to their trade union struggle and capacity to survive hardship. This moral conviction based on their deeply grounded belief in justice and equality gave strength to their fight, the strength to resist the proposed wage cut as well as to publicly challenge and openly criticise their Union, their Union's Members of Parliament, and publicly argue with the Board of Guardians over their interpretation and application of the Poor Law.

This moral and political philosophy based on equality and fair-play was so deeply embedded in the population of this part of West Yorkshire that the Parliamentary constituency of Hemsworth was known as *'The Jewel in Labours Crown'*, the Parliamentary seat where they did not need to count the number of votes for Labour:

'They Weighed Them.'

In these times of career politicians and organised lobby groups, characterised in many ways by *Dumbing-Down* and *Opinion*

Forming news media, it is reassuring to know that the ordinary person even without the benefits of a university education, has within them the ability and ingenuity to organise and argue at every level in society for what they believe is right; even in those cases where the obstacles and opponents appear to be powerful, formidable and well organised. Such characteristics are essential for the inhabitants of any liberal democratic society such as the one we cherish.

Appendix 1

Guide to the meaning of the terms used. My interpretation of the words may not be perfect however they make sense in the context in which they are used.

'Getting Price'	was the amount paid to the miner for each ton of coal recovered.
'Played'	Seems to be used in two contexts: i. The pit *'played'* ie. The pit was idle. ii. The man *'played'* ie. He took a day off work.
'Pulled'	the Engineman misjudged the stopping place for the pit cage and drew the cage up into the winding gear.
'Old pit'	This would refer to the Shafton seam.
'Nipsey Fund'	comprised of the sum of monies donated and collected by voluntary means to assist the miners. The *Nipsey fund* was calculated on a weekly basis and distributed amongst the miners and their families as *Nipsey money.*
'Stood Over'	Left undecided.

Appendix 2

Prior to the decimal currency units we now use, Pounds, Shillings and Pence was the common currency. For those of us too young to remember this currency I have included a simple conversion table below.

Old Money Value	Common Name	Present Coinage
£1	Pound – 240 pennies	£1
10/-	Ten Shillings – 120 pennies or Ten bob note	50p
5/-	Five Shillings – 60 pennies	None
2/6d	Half a Crown – 30 pennies	None
2/-	Two Shillings – 24 pennies or Florin	10p
1/-	Shilling – 12 pennies	5p
6d	Sixpence – 6 pennies or Tanner	None
3d	Threepence – 3 pennies	None
1d	Penny – 1 penny	1p
½d	Half-penny – ½ of a penny	None
¼d	Farthing – ¼ of a penny	None

Lightning Source UK Ltd.
Milton Keynes UK
UKHW041930200121
377415UK00001B/33

9 781425 168582